100 GREAT SOUPS

ORLA BRODERICK

PHOTOGRAPHS BY
ROBIN MATTHEWS

WEIDENFELD
& NICOLSON
LONDON

CONTENTS

A WELL-STOCKED KITCHEN

You will find most of the ingredients I use regularly are fairly straightforward, with a few little luxuries thrown in. It is amazing how many unexpected situations you can take in your stride if your kitchen is well stocked. Obviously, you don't need to have all of the following ingredients all of the time, but you'll find that if you cook regularly none of them should go to waste. Keep ingredients in the storecupboard in small quantities and make an effort to use them before their sell-by date. Always use the best quality you can afford – I buy organic or free-range produce whenever possible. Try to buy vegetables when they are in season; not only will they be the freshest and tastiest, but they will save you money as well.

IN THE STORECUPBOARD

BAY LEAVES

CANS OF VARIOUS BEANS AND CHICKPEAS

BOTTLES OF SAUCES AND PASTES, SUCH AS CHILLI
    AND GARLIC SAUCE OR HARISSA; SOY SAUCE;
    TABASCO SAUCE; THAI FISH SAUCE (*NAM PLA*);
    WORCESTERSHIRE SAUCE

CHINESE NOODLES

PLAIN FLOUR

CLEAR HONEY

BOTTLES OF EXTRA VIRGIN OLIVE OIL,
    SUNFLOWER OIL AND SESAME OIL

FINE SEA SALT

GROUND SPICES, SUCH AS CURRY POWDER,
    PAPRIKA AND TURMERIC

WHOLE SPICES, SUCH AS SMALL DRIED CHILLIES;
    CORIANDER AND CUMIN SEEDS; NUTMEGS;
    BLACK AND WHITE PEPPERCORNS; STAR ANISE

A SELECTION OF STOCK CUBES

A SELECTION OF SUGARS, INCLUDING LIGHT
    MUSCOVADO AND CASTER

CANS OF CHOPPED TOMATOES AND TUBES
    OR JARS OF TOMATO PURÉE

TORTILLA CHIPS

IN THE REFRIGERATOR

BACON LARDONS

BUTTER

CHEDDAR AND PARMESAN CHEESES

CRÈME FRAÎCHE

DOUBLE CREAM

EGGS

SPRING ONIONS

BOTTLE OF DRY WHITE WINE

NATURAL YOGHURT

IN THE FREEZER

BREAD

PEAS

PUFF PASTRY

SPINACH

CARTONS OF SHOP-BOUGHT AND HOMEMADE
    (IF YOU'RE REALLY ORGANIZED!) CHICKEN
    AND VEGETABLE STOCKS

WHITE CRAB MEAT

IN THE VEGETABLE BASKET

CARROTS

CELERY

FRESH CHILLIES

GARLIC

GINGER

LEEKS

LEMONS

LIMES

ONIONS

RED PEPPERS

POTATOES

SHALLOTS

ON THE WINDOW SILL

I would be lost without the selection of fresh herbs I have growing so conveniently on my window sill. I also always keep my tomatoes on the window sill, as it helps them continue to ripen and develop flavour. The selection of herbs I recommend are:

BASIL	FLAT-LEAF PARSLEY
CHERVIL	SAGE
CHIVES	TARRAGON
MINT	THYME

EQUIPMENT

With the exception of a good sharp knife, a decent chopping board and a large, deep pan (preferably with a tight-fitting lid),

very little specialist equipment is necessary to prepare and cook the soups from this book.

However, the following items definitely have their uses:

FOOD PROCESSOR
I often purée soups and a food processor does this perfectly, even if you do have to do it in batches. If you have the space, give your food processor a permanent place on your worktop, as not only does it save time but you will find you use it more.

HAND-HELD LIQUIDIZER
I think this is one of the most practical pieces of electrical equipment on the market today. I use it all the time for puréeing soups. Just hold the liquidizer directly in the pan, which also saves on the washing up! Most of the brands also come with a detachable small bowl, which is the perfect size for blending small amounts of ingredients, such as when making pestos.

SIEVE
A good-quality, fine sieve should last you a lifetime. It allows you to strain your finished soups for a much smoother, velvety texture. It simply removes all of the tough, fibrous pieces without taking away any of the flavour. Just use a little elbow grease and the back of a wooden spoon to work the ingredients through the fine mesh. Occasionally I recommend passing clear, consommé-style soups or any type of shellfish cooking liquid through a muslin lining in the sieve, which will strain out even finer particles.

VEGETABLE MILL
Otherwise known as a mouli-legumes, this can be a most useful gadget in the art of soup making. It is actually a sophisticated sieve with a built-in masher that has three different sized metal discs for varying degrees of puréeing. It also normally comes with folding feet that secure it over your pan or bowl and help to hold it steady. Vegetable mills are relatively inexpensive and there is no danger of them breaking down, but the downside is that they can be difficult to clean.

LADLE
A good-sized ladle is invaluable when you need to transfer soup into a food processor in batches. It allows you to control the amount of solids and liquid that go into each batch. It is also useful when serving soup as it helps you judge the right quantity per person.

DRAINING/SLOTTED SPOON
This is useful for lifting cooked fish and shellfish or dumplings and wontons out of hot liquids to prevent overcooking. It also makes it easier to remove a bouquet garni or bay leaf.

SKIMMER
Use this to take off any scum and excess fat that rises to the surface of your stock pot, resulting in a clearer finished broth. Its advantage is that it takes only the bare amount and allows all the liquid to drain back into the pan.

THE RECIPES

THE BASICS

The majority of recipes in this section are for garnishes and other simple ideas to improve the flavour of your soups.

Most are a last-minute optional extra to add a texture variation and something pleasing to the eye.

They also give you infinite scope to vary and personalize the recipes.

CHICKEN STOCK

It is important to taste stock regularly while it cooks as it will eventually reach a point where the flavour stops improving. This happens after 2 to 3 hours. Makes about 900ml/1½ pints.

1 chicken carcass with scraps of skin	*2 leeks, chopped*
and the giblets, if available	*1 bay leaf*
1 onion, unpeeled and quartered	*1 fresh thyme sprig*
2 celery sticks, chopped	*15g/½oz fresh parsley or tarragon stalks*
1 large carrot, chopped	*6 black peppercorns*

Place all the ingredients in a large saucepan. Just cover with about 1.7 litres/3 pints cold water and bring to the boil, skimming off any fat or scum that rises to the surface.

Reduce the heat and simmer for 2–3 hours, occasionally skimming off any excess fat that rises to the top. Strain through a fine sieve into a tall container and leave to cool. If you have time, chill in the fridge and lift off any fat that sets on the surface. The stock will keep for 1–2 days in the fridge, or you can divide it into tubs and freeze until ready to use.

VEGETABLE STOCK

This stock is wonderfully fragrant and is worth making in big batches as it freezes well. You might want to dilute it before using, depending on how long it was left to infuse. Makes about 900ml/1½ pints.

2 tbsp olive oil	*1 bay leaf*
1 large onion, chopped	*1 star anise*
2 celery sticks, chopped	*1 tsp coriander seeds*
1 small fennel bulb, chopped	*½ tsp white peppercorns, crushed*
2 large carrots, chopped	*25g/1oz bunch fresh mixed herbs*
1 garlic bulb, sliced in half	*300ml/10fl oz dry white wine*

Heat the oil in a large saucepan. Add the onion and fry until softened but not browned. Stir in the remaining vegetables and bay leaf and cook, stirring, for a minute or so. Pour in 900ml/1½ pints water and bring to the boil, then reduce the heat and simmer for 30 minutes.

Add the star anise, coriander seeds and peppercorns and simmer for 10 minutes, then add the herbs and wine and simmer for another 5 minutes. Remove from the heat, cover and leave to infuse in a cold place – the flavour improves for up to 48 hours. Strain through a fine sieve and use as required. This will keep in the fridge for another 1–2 days, or you can divide it into tubs and freeze until ready to use.

FISH STOCK

I have not included salt in this recipe as the stock is greatly reduced so could become too salty. The seasoning should therefore be added when making the soup. Fishmongers often have bones for sale (but not on display) so don't be afraid to ask. Bones from flat fish, such as sole, turbot and brill, are the best to use. Makes about 900ml/1½ pints.

1.5kg/3lb fish bones, including heads	*1 bay leaf*
2 celery sticks, chopped	*15g/½oz fresh mixed parsley, tarragon*
2 leeks, chopped	*and chervil stalks*
1 large onion, chopped	*6 black peppercorns*
1 large carrot, chopped	

Soak the fish bones in cold water for 30 minutes. Drain, wash well and roughly chop. Place in a large saucepan with all the remaining ingredients. Just cover with about 1.5 litres/3 pints cold water and bring to the boil, skimming off any scum that rises to the surface.

Reduce the heat and simmer for 30 minutes without boiling, occasionally skimming the top, if necessary. Remove from the heat and leave to cool completely, which will take 3–4 hours.

Strain the stock through a fine sieve into a tall container, then if you have time place in the fridge overnight to settle. The next day skim off any scum that has settled on the top. This will keep for 1–2 days in the fridge, or you can divide it into tubs, discarding the sediment that has settled at the bottom, and freeze until ready to use.

ROUILLE

This fiery, hot Provençal sauce is traditionally served with fish soups. It can be served separately in little bowls so that it can be used as a dip, spread on to croûtons or just whisked directly into the soup. Makes about 150g/5oz.

1 red pepper
1 small slice stale bread
2 garlic cloves, crushed

1 mild red chilli, seeded and chopped
Salt and freshly ground black pepper
6 tbsp extra virgin olive oil

Preheat the grill. Place the pepper on the grill rack and grill for 20–30 minutes until blackened and blistered, turning regularly. Place in a polythene bag, secure with a knot and allow to steam in its own heat for 10 minutes. Remove from the bag, peel, seed and chop the flesh, reserving any juices.

Meanwhile, soak the bread in a little water for about 5 minutes, then squeeze out the excess. Place in a food processor with the pepper flesh, garlic and chilli. Season generously and whizz to a paste. With the motor running, gradually pour in the oil to make a smooth, shiny sauce. Transfer to a bowl and cover with clingfilm or store in a screw-topped jar. This will keep in the fridge for up to 1 week. Return to room temperature before using.

PESTOS

These are vibrant, pungent sauces that can be drizzled into soups to garnish or just stirred in at the last moment for extra flavour. I also like to spread them on to croûtes (page 14) or simply use as a dip. Experiment using the suggestions below, then make up your own – the variations are endless.

TRADITIONAL ITALIAN PESTO
Makes about 150ml/5fl oz.

15g/¹/₂oz pine nuts
25g/1oz fresh basil leaves
15g/¹/₂oz freshly grated Parmesan

1 garlic clove, chopped
6 tbsp extra virgin olive oil
Sea salt and freshly ground black pepper

Toast the pine nuts in a small frying pan until lightly golden, then remove from the heat and leave to cool completely. When cold, place in a food processor with the basil, Parmesan, garlic and olive oil. Season generously and whizz for 30 seconds.

Scrape down inside the bowl with a rubber spatula and whizz again for 30 seconds. Transfer to a bowl and cover with clingfilm or store in a screw-topped jar. This will keep in the fridge for up to 1 week; top up with a little olive oil each time you use it to keep the vibrant colour.

* Use a combination of basil, flat-leaf parsley and rocket leaves for a more pronounced peppery flavour. This is very good with all types of tomato soups.

* Replace the pine nuts with walnuts and use all flat-leaf parsley for a more robust taste. This combination is good spread on to croûtes, topped with sliced goats' cheese and grilled until bubbling; float in the soup to serve.

* Replace the Parmesan with watercress and, instead of the basil, use a combination of chives, tarragon, chervil and flat-leaf parsley for a sophisticated flavour, which is great with any fish soup.

* Add 2 peeled, seeded and diced plum tomatoes to the basic mixture. This is excellent with minestrone-style soups.

SALSAS

Use only the freshest of ingredients when making salsas and keep them separate until just before you are ready to serve. I like salsas either piled in tiny mounds on tortilla chips which can then be served with the soup or floating on top, or scattered directly over any chilled summer soup.

SALSA FRESCA
Makes about 150g/5oz.

2 large plum tomatoes, peeled, seeded and diced
1 small red onion, finely diced
1 garlic clove, finely chopped
1 mild red chilli, seeded and finely chopped

Juice of 1 lime
2 tbsp extra virgin olive oil
2 tbsp chopped fresh flat-leaf parsley
Pinch of sugar
Salt and freshly ground black pepper

Place the tomatoes, onion, garlic, chilli, lime juice, oil and parsley in a bowl. Add the sugar and season generously, then mix gently to combine. Serve at room temperature.

* For a spicy kick, add ¹/₄ teaspoon each ground coriander and cumin and replace the parsley with fresh coriander. Use in robust, bean-based soups.

* For a tropical salsa, replace the tomatoes with 1 large diced mango. This is fantastic with most kinds of Asian or oriental soups, especially the fish ones.

* Replace the tomatoes with sweetcorn kernels and the parsley with fresh coriander. This is perfect to serve with any Mexican-style soup.

* For a milder Mediterranean flavour, omit the red onion and chilli and replace the lime juice with a splash of balsamic vinegar and the fresh parsley with basil.

Clockwise from top: Salsa Fresca, Rouille, Traditional Italian Pesto

TO THICKEN SOUP

Plenty of soups don't need thickening; however, some need something to pull all the ingredients and the texture together.

REDUCTION

Soups that don't include cream, yoghurt or eggs can be thickened easily by reduction. Simply simmer the soup, uncovered, for 20–30 minutes, keeping an eye on the progress until you have reached the required consistency and to make sure nothing is sticking to the bottom of the pan. However, don't forget that this process will also intensify the flavours, so leave adding any salt until the end.

OLIVE OIL

One of the best ways to thicken a vegetable soup once it is cooked is to stir in a couple of tablespoons of extra virgin olive oil and just return the soup to the boil, then remove from the heat. You can repeat this process a couple of times with excellent results and, surprisingly, no trace of oiliness.

EGGS AND CREAM

Egg yolks mixed with stock, milk or cream and added to the soup just before serving will thicken and enrich it beyond belief. Although you need a certain amount of heat to cook the eggs, whatever you do, don't allow the soup to boil or they will curdle. Simply add 1 or 2 egg yolks to 50ml/2fl oz of your chosen liquid for every 600ml/1 pint soup. Add a ladleful of the hot soup to the egg yolk mixture, mixing until well combined, then stir the mixture back into the soup and gently warm through.

GROUND NUTS

Ground almonds, hazelnuts and walnuts are traditionally used to thicken soups in Spain and Mexico. Stir about 50g/2oz into a full quantity of soup and simmer for a few minutes until thickened.

GARNISHES

CROÛTONS

Cut the crusts off 100g/4oz firm-crumbed bread and cut into 5mm/¼in cubes, diamonds or hearts. Heat 4 tablespoons oil or melt 50g/2oz unsalted butter, lard or fat in a large frying pan. Add the croûtons and cook gently for 5–10 minutes, tossing and turning occasionally until golden. For a healthier version, preheat the oven to 190°C/375°F/Gas 5. Place the croûtons in a bowl with 1 tablespoon olive oil and stir gently until coated, then spread out in a single layer on a baking sheet. Bake for 8–10 minutes until crisp and golden. Drain croûtons on kitchen paper before serving. Croûtons can be stored in an airtight tin or polythene bag for a few days.

* Garlic croûtons: mix 2 crushed garlic cloves with the oil before tossing it through the bread cubes prior to cooking.

* Parmesan croûtons: mix 2 tablespoons freshly grated Parmesan with the oil before tossing it through the bread cubes.

* Anchovy croûtons: mash a drained 50g/2oz can of anchovy fillets into the oil until disintegrated, then mix with the bread cubes.

* Olive croûtons: mix 2 teaspoons black or green olive paste (from a jar) with the oil, then mix with the bread cubes.

* Bacon croûtons: fry 100g/4oz diced pancetta or streaky bacon until crisp, then mix with the finished croûtons at the last minute.

CROÛTES

Place thin slices of day-old French bread or ciabatta on a baking sheet and either bake in a preheated oven (at its lowest setting) or toast under the grill until dry but not browned. Rub both sides with a peeled garlic clove and drizzle some extra virgin olive oil on top. For toasted cheese croûtes, top the bread with grated cheese before cooking. Alternatively, you can spread the croûtes with any of the flavour variations above prior to cooking.

PASTRY PUFFS

Preheat the oven to 180°C/350°F/Gas 4. Stamp or cut out shapes – hearts or stars and moons – from ready-rolled puff pastry. Arrange on a parchment-lined baking sheet and sprinkle with freshly grated Parmesan, poppy seeds, celery seeds, a dusting of paprika or chopped fresh herbs. Bake for 5–10 minutes, depending on the size of the shapes. Cool on a wire rack and float in bowls of soup to serve.

CHEESE GARNISHES

* Grate some Cheddar or Gruyère and sprinkle it over each bowl of soup just before serving. Alternatively, swirl in a little extra virgin olive oil and scatter a few shavings of Parmesan or pecorino on top.

* Cut some quick-melting cheese, such as Gruyère, manchego, fontina or mozzarella into little cubes and stir into soup just before serving.

CARROT SPAGHETTI

Cut 2 large carrots into neat rectangular blocks and then cut into long fine strips – a mandolin will do this very well. Place in a saucepan and cover with cold water. Add a knob of butter and a pinch of salt, bring to a simmer and then simmer until just tender. Drain and use at once.

CRISPY SEAWEED

Very finely shred leafy greens, such as cabbage, spinach or curly kale, and deep-fry in batches at 190°C/375°F for 1–2 minutes until crispy. Drain on kitchen paper and season with a little salt and sugar.

VEGETABLE HAIR

This works well with leeks, carrots, parsnips, beetroots, celeriac and ginger. You can use them individually or in combination. Peel and cut the vegetables of your choice into julienne strips (use a mandolin if you've got one) and deep-fry at 190°C/375°F for 30–60 seconds until crisp. Drain on kitchen paper and season with coarse sea salt.

VEGETABLE CRISPS

Root vegetables, especially parsnips, potatoes and beetroots, make fantastic crisps. Peel and cut the vegetables into wafer-thin rounds (use a mandolin if you've got one), rinse and pat dry. Deep-fry at 190°C/375°F for 1–2 minutes until crisp and lightly golden. Drain well on kitchen paper. Pile up on dollops of soured cream.

CRISPY ONIONS

Cut the onions in half lengthways and then thinly slice. Drain between sheets of kitchen paper for about 30 minutes to draw out moisture. Heat about 1cm/½in oil in a wok or large frying pan and stir-fry the onions for 15–20 minutes until richly brown, taking care that they don't burn. Sprinkle over spoonfuls of yoghurt.

DEEP-FRIED BASIL

This has a wonderful translucent look. Rinse basil leaves and pat dry. Heat 50ml/2fl oz olive oil until very hot, but not smoking. Remove from the heat and drop in the basil leaves for a few seconds. Remove with a slotted spoon and drain on kitchen paper.

GUACAMOLE

Dice a large, ripe avocado and mix with 2 peeled, seeded and diced tomatoes, a couple of tablespoons of chopped fresh coriander, 4 finely chopped spring onions, 1 seeded and diced red chilli and a little crushed garlic. Season to taste.

SALSA VERDE

Place 15g/½oz flat-leaf parsley leaves, 12 basil leaves, 6 mint leaves, 1 chopped garlic clove, 1 tablespoon rinsed capers and 2 chopped

anchovy fillets in a mini-blender and whizz until just blended. Place in a bowl and gradually whisk in 1 teaspoon each of red wine vinegar, lemon juice and Dijon mustard and 4 tablespoons olive oil. Season well.

MINT RELISH

Place 15g/½oz fresh mint leaves, 1 seeded and chopped green chilli, 2 chopped spring onions, ½ teaspoon freshly grated root ginger, a squeeze of lemon juice and a good pinch of salt and sugar in a mini-blender. Add a couple of tablespoons of water and whizz to a purée.

BASIL PURÉE

This can be made in a mini-blender but I find the pestle and mortar helps to keep the vibrant colour for longer. Place 15g/½oz fresh basil leaves in a mortar with a good pinch of fine sea salt. Grind for 1–2 minutes with a pestle and then work in 2 tablespoons extra virgin olive oil and 1 teaspoon balsamic vinegar. Season to taste.

BLACK MUSTARD SEED AND ONION TARKA

Heat 4 tablespoons sunflower oil in a frying pan and add 75g/3oz dried onion flakes and 1 teaspoon black mustard seeds. Stir-fry for 1 minute, then drain well on kitchen paper. Serve hot or cold, sprinkled over a simple vegetable or lentil soup to give it an extra dimension.

FLAVOURED BUTTERS

These are great cut into thin slices and served on top of soup. I find they enrich and enhance the existing flavours. They can be made in advance and keep for 1 week in the fridge or 2 months in the freezer. Each recipe makes 150g/5oz in total.

TARRAGON BUTTER

150ml/5fl oz dry white wine
2 shallots, finely chopped
100g/4oz unsalted butter, softened

2 tbsp chopped fresh tarragon
Fine sea salt and freshly ground
black pepper

Place the wine and shallots in a small saucepan and boil fast until the wine has almost disappeared. Leave to cool completely, then gradually beat into the butter with the tarragon. Season to taste. Shape and roll in a piece of parchment paper to make a cylinder. Chill for 2 hours until firm, then use as required.

PIQUANT BUTTER

2 garlic cloves, crushed
1 tbsp capers, rinsed and finely chopped
2 tbsp chopped fresh flat-leaf parsley

100g/4oz unsalted butter, softened
Fine sea salt and freshly ground
black pepper

Beat the garlic, capers and flat-leaf parsley into the butter and season to taste. Shape and roll as before.

CHILLI AND LIME BUTTER

2 mild red chillies, seeded and
finely chopped
Grated zest and juice of 1 small lime
1 tbsp snipped fresh chives

100g/4oz unsalted butter
Fine sea salt and freshly ground
black pepper

Beat the chillies, lime zest and juice and chives into the butter and season to taste. Shape and roll as before.

BLUE CHEESE BUTTER

75g/3oz blue cheese, such as
Roquefort or Stilton
1 tbsp chopped fresh flat-leaf parsley

50g/2oz unsalted butter, softened
Fine sea salt and freshly ground
black pepper

Beat the cheese and flat-leaf parsley into the butter and season to taste. Shape and roll as before.

FLAVOURED COOLERS

These are designed to give a contrasting texture, flavour and temperature to a soup, as well as acting as an attractive garnish. They work well with gutsy, well-flavoured and spicy soups. Just spoon into the centre of the soup; if you wish you can swirl it out to make a delicate feather pattern, using a cocktail stick.

SWEET PEPPER CREAM

Grill a red or yellow pepper until blackened and blistered (see recipe for Rouille on page 12 for full instructions), then peel and remove the seeds. Purée the flesh in a mini-blender and then press through a sieve into 50ml/2fl oz unwhipped double cream. Season to taste.

SOURED CREAM COOLER

Mix together 150ml/5fl oz soured cream, 2 peeled, seeded and diced plum tomatoes and 2 heaped tablespoons shredded basil. Season generously.

HERB CREAM

Whip 150ml/5fl oz double cream until thick but not stiff. Season generously and stir in 3 tablespoons chopped fresh herbs of your choice (if using rosemary or thyme, add only very small amounts, as they have a much stronger, more pronounced flavour than other fresh herbs).

MINTED YOGHURT COOLER

Mix together 150g/5oz natural yoghurt, 1 crushed garlic clove and 2 tablespoons chopped fresh mint. Season with a pinch of salt.

LIME-INFUSED YOGHURT

This would also work well with oranges or lemons. Mix together 300g/10oz Greek strained yoghurt wih the finely grated zest and juice of 1 lime. Set aside and leave to infuse for 30 minutes. Season generously and add a pinch of freshly grated root ginger and 2 teaspoons snipped fresh chives.

SAFFRON MASCARPONE

I love this with any potato or seafood soup. Soak a good pinch of saffron strands in 1 tablespoon hot water. Beat into 250g/9oz mascarpone and season generously.

AIOLI

Have all of the ingredients at room temperature. Place 1 peeled and chopped garlic clove in a mortar and use a pestle to pound to a paste with a pinch of salt, then work in 1 egg yolk. Add 150ml/5fl oz olive oil, drop by drop, until well combined. Stir in 1 tablespoon white wine vinegar and season well.

Clockwise from top right: Piquant Butter, Tarragon Butter,
Chilli and Lime Butter, Blue Cheese Butter

HOT & SPICY

These recipes come from all around the world and are for anyone who likes a bit of a kick in their food. 'Hotness' is such a matter of personal taste that I recommend you always use chillies with caution, as they vary enormously in strength.

All recipes serve 4–6.

FIERY LENTIL SOUP

The spices give this nutritious soup an excellent flavour. It is similar to a traditional dhal, and would make a good starter for an Indian meal if reduced to make a slightly thicker purée.

1 tbsp sunflower oil
1 large onion, chopped
4 garlic cloves, crushed
2 tsp ground turmeric
2 tsp garam masala
1 bay leaf
6 cardamom pods, crushed
225g/8oz red or orange lentils, washed

900ml/1½ pints vegetable stock
Salt and freshly ground black pepper
225g/8oz fresh spinach leaves, roughly chopped
Juice of 1 lime
Unflavoured natural yoghurt and chopped fresh coriander, to serve

Heat the oil in a large pan. Add the onion and fry for 5–6 minutes until golden brown. Stir in the garlic, turmeric, garam masala, bay leaf and cardamom pods and cook gently for 1 minute until the spices are lightly toasted.

Add the lentils to the pan with the stock and season well. Simmer for about 20 minutes, or until the lentils are just tender. Stir in the spinach and cook for a further 5 minutes. Season to taste and add the lime juice. Ladle into bowls and add a spoonful of yoghurt and some coriander. Serve at once.

GARLIC BREAD SOUP

This is a great recipe to have to hand if you haven't got much in. I grow all my own herbs on the kitchen window sill and even have a chilli plant which produces all year round.

4 tbsp olive oil
100g/4oz pancetta or streaky bacon lardons, diced
10 garlic cloves, finely chopped
2 red chillies, seeded and finely chopped
1 heaped tsp fresh thyme leaves

½ tsp chopped fresh sage
1 tsp paprika
1.2 litres/2 pints chicken or vegetable stock
6 thick slices country bread, crusts removed and cut into cubes
Salt and freshly ground black pepper

Heat the olive oil in a large pan. Add the pancetta and cook for about 5 minutes until lightly golden and crispy. Stir in the garlic, chilli, thyme and sage and cook for another few minutes, then stir in the paprika. Pour in the stock, add the bread and simmer for another 10 minutes, or until the bread has broken down and thickened the soup. Season to taste, ladle into bowls and serve at once.

CHICKEN, COCONUT AND GALANGAL SOUP

Coconut milk, one of my favourite ingredients, makes a fantastic creamy base for all the other robust flavours in this Asian-style soup. It is so simple it literally takes minutes to prepare.

900ml/1½ pints chicken stock
4 kaffir lime leaves
5cm/2in piece galangal, peeled and cut into matchsticks
4 tbsp Thai fish sauce
Juice of 2 lemons

225g/8oz skinless, boneless chicken breasts, thinly sliced
400ml/14fl oz coconut milk
Good pinch dried chilli flakes
4 tbsp fresh coriander leaves

Place the stock in a large pan with the lime leaves, galangal, fish sauce and lemon juice. Bring to the boil, stirring continuously. Reduce the heat and simmer for 5 minutes until the galangal is tender. Add the chicken and coconut milk and continue to cook over a high heat for 2 minutes, or until the chicken is cooked through and tender. Add the dried chilli flakes and coriander and cook for another 20 seconds, then ladle into bowls and serve at once.

JAPANESE MISO SOUP

Instant fish stock (*dashi-no-moto*) and the other ingredients you need for this recipe are readily available in Asian food stores and some supermarkets. There are a number of different types of miso and all make good soup; flavours range from slightly sweet to slightly bitter.

2 tbsp sunflower oil
225g/8oz fresh shiitake mushrooms, sliced
1.2 litres/2 pints reconstituted Japanese soup stock (dashi-no-moto) or light vegetable stock

75g/3oz young leaf spinach
4 heaped tbsp miso
Dark soy sauce, to taste
Lemon rind slivers, to garnish

Heat the oil in a pan. Add the mushrooms and sauté for about 5 minutes until tender. Pour in the stock and bring to the boil. Reduce the heat, add the spinach and simmer for a few minutes until the spinach has wilted and the mushrooms are completely tender. Blend a little of the stock with the miso and stir into the pan. Bring almost to the boil, season with soy sauce and ladle into bowls. Garnish with the lemon rind and serve at once.

Above: Curried Parsnip Soup

CHICKEN NOODLE SOUP

The flavour idea for this comes from Thai cooking, where spicy flavours are cut with the acidity of lemons or limes. The secret is in the balance and no one element should dominate.

250g/9oz vermicelli rice noodles
2 tbsp sunflower oil
2 large skinless, boneless chicken breasts,
cut into thin strips
2 garlic cloves, crushed
2 tbsp Thai red curry paste

1.2 litres/2 pints chicken stock
1 head of pak choi, thinly sliced
1 bunch spring onions, thinly sliced
3 tbsp light soy sauce
Juice of 1 lemon
Good handful of fresh mint leaves

Plunge the noodles into a large pan of boiling salted water, remove from the heat and set aside for 2 minutes, or according to the packet instructions. Drain and rinse under cold running water. Set aside.

Heat the oil in a large pan. Add the chicken and cook over a high heat for 2–3 minutes, stirring until lightly browned. Stir in the garlic and curry paste and cook for another minute, stirring. Pour in the stock and bring to the boil. Reduce the heat and simmer for 5 minutes, or until the chicken is completely cooked through and tender.

Stir in the pak choi and spring onions and cook for another minute or so until the greens have just wilted. Add the soy sauce and lemon juice and remove from the heat. Divide the noodles between serving bowls, scatter over the mint leaves and ladle in the hot soup. Serve at once.

CURRIED PARSNIP SOUP

Use a fresh, good-quality curry powder for this soup and not one that has been stuck at the back of the cupboard for the last six months.

50g/2oz unsalted butter
1 onion, finely chopped
1 garlic clove, finely chopped
2 parsnips, chopped
1 potato, diced
2 tsp medium curry powder

900ml/1½ pints chicken or
vegetable stock
Salt and freshly ground black pepper
150ml/5fl oz double cream
Croûtons (page 14) and snipped
fresh chives, to garnish

Melt the butter in a large pan. Add the onion and garlic and cook for 2–3 minutes until just beginning to soften. Add the parsnips and potato, turn to coat in the butter, cover the pan and cook for 10 minutes, stirring once or twice.

Stir the curry powder into the vegetable mixture and cook for another minute or so, stirring. Pour in the stock, season generously and bring to the boil. Reduce the heat and simmer for 40 minutes, or until the parsnips are completely tender and the soup has thickened.

Leave the soup to cool a little, then purée in batches in a food processor or with a hand-held liquidizer. To serve, stir in the cream and reheat gently. Season to taste, ladle into bowls and garnish with the croûtons and chives.

SWEET POTATO SPLASH

The skins of sweet potatoes can be white, pink or purple, and the flesh is either creamy white or orange, but they all taste the same.

50g/2oz unsalted butter
1 large onion, finely chopped
675g/1½lb sweet potatoes,
peeled and diced
1 tsp fresh thyme leaves,
plus extra to garnish

Salt and freshly ground black pepper
½ tsp ground allspice
2 red birds' eye chillies, seeded and
finely chopped
900ml/1½ pints chicken or vegetable stock
200ml/7fl oz crème fraîche

Melt the butter in a large heavy-based pan with a tight-fitting lid. Add the onion and cook for 2–3 minutes until just beginning to soften. Stir in the sweet potatoes until well coated. Add the thyme and season generously, then place a parchment paper circle directly on top to keep in the steam. Cover the pan and sweat over a low heat for about 10 minutes until the sweet potatoes have softened but not coloured.

Remove the lid and the paper and stir in the allspice and chillies, then cook for another minute, stirring. Pour in the stock and bring to the boil. Reduce the heat and simmer for another 10 minutes, or until the sweet potatoes are completely tender. Purée the soup in batches in a food processor or with a hand-held liquidizer. Pour back into the pan, season to taste and add two-thirds of the crème fraîche. Reheat gently, then ladle into bowls and add spoonfuls of the remaining crème fraîche. Garnish with thyme leaves and serve at once.

THAI MIXED FISH SOUP

This is the basic method for making Thai *tom yam* soup so you can experiment with your choice of fish and shellfish. Try it with a mixture of scallops, mussels, squid and crab claws.

*1.2 litres/2 pints chicken or
vegetable stock
2.5cm/1in piece peeled galangal,
chopped
2 lemon grass stalks, lightly crushed
and chopped
3 kaffir lime leaves, finely chopped
1 tbsp grilled chilli oil (tom yam sauce)
2 red bird's eye chillies, seeded and
finely chopped*

*Juice of 1 lemon
4 tbsp Thai fish sauce
1/2 tsp sugar
350g/12oz firm white fish fillets,
skinned and cut into chunks
100g/4oz raw tiger prawns,
peeled and de-veined
4 spring onions, finely chopped
2 tbsp roughly chopped fresh coriander*

Place the stock in a pan with the galangal, lemon grass, lime leaves and chilli oil and bring to the boil. Reduce the heat and simmer for 15 minutes, then strain into a clean pan.

Add the chillies, lemon juice, fish sauce and sugar to the flavoured stock and simmer for 2 minutes, then add the fish, prawns and spring onions and simmer for a further 2–3 minutes until the fish and prawns are just tender. Ladle into soup bowls and sprinkle over the coriander to serve.

CHINESE PRAWN-BALL SOUP

This refreshing soup is made rather glamorous by the addition of the prawn balls. Although they are expensive to make using the raw tiger prawns, the flavour makes it well worth it.

*Groundnut oil for deep-frying
450g/1lb raw tiger prawns, peeled
and de-veined
25g/1oz pork fat or lard
1 egg white
2 spring onions, finely chopped
1 green chilli, seeded and finely chopped
1 tsp freshly grated root ginger*

*Salt and freshly ground black pepper
1.4 litres/2½ pints chicken stock
3 tbsp Shaoxing rice wine or dry sherry
2 tbsp light soy sauce
1 tsp sugar
2 tsp sesame oil
225g/8oz fresh watercress,
large stalks removed*

Heat 5cm/2in oil in a pan to 190°C/375°F. Meanwhile, place the prawns, pork fat, egg white, spring onions, chilli and ginger in a food processor. Add 1 teaspoon salt and ¼ teaspoon pepper and whizz briefly to a smooth paste. Form spoonfuls of the paste into balls, about 2.5cm/1in in diameter. Carefully drop the balls into the heated oil and deep-fry for 3–4 minutes until puffed up and golden brown. Drain well on kitchen paper.

Place the stock in a large pan with the wine or sherry, soy sauce and sugar. Bring to a simmer and cook for 3 minutes. Add the prawn balls and cook for another 2 minutes. Stir in the sesame oil, season to taste and remove from the heat. Divide the watercress between the serving bowls, ladle over the soup and prawn balls and serve at once.

ASIAN CHICKEN AND SWEETCORN SOUP

This is a variation on an old favourite that has stood the test of time. It appears in some form on every Chinese take-away menu in the country, but I really like the fresh flavours of this version.

*2 tbsp sunflower oil
2 garlic cloves, finely chopped
2.5cm/1in piece fresh root ginger,
finely chopped
2 green bird's eye chillies, seeded and
finely chopped
2 skinless, boneless chicken breasts,
finely sliced
2 tbsp cornflour*

*1.2 litres/2 pints chicken stock
225g/8oz sweetcorn kernels
2 eggs
Juice of 1 lemon
Salt and freshly ground black pepper
About 2 tsp dark soy sauce
2 tbsp roughly chopped fresh coriander
Prawn crackers, to serve*

Heat the oil in a large pan. Add the garlic, ginger and chillies and stir-fry for 30 seconds or so. Add the chicken and stir-fry for 3–4 minutes until well sealed. Blend the cornflour with a little of the stock and add to the pan with the remaining stock and the sweetcorn. Bring to the boil, stirring continuously. Reduce the heat and simmer gently for about 5 minutes.

Beat together the eggs and lemon juice and slowly trickle into the soup, stirring with a chopstick or fork to make egg strands. Season to taste and pour into serving bowls. Add a drizzle of soy sauce and scatter over the coriander. Serve at once with prawn crackers.

Above: Thai Mixed Fish Soup

MOROCCAN CHICKPEA SOUP

It really makes a huge difference in flavour if you grind your own spices. If you haven't got a mini-blender, a pestle and mortar works just as well – it just takes a bit more time.

½ small cinnamon stick	1.2 litres/2 pints chicken or vegetable stock
2 whole cloves	450g/1lb small salad potatoes, quartered
½ tsp each yellow mustard, cumin and	400g/14oz can chickpeas, drained
coriander seeds	and rinsed
2 tbsp olive oil	Salt and freshly ground black pepper
1 onion, chopped	50g/2oz spinach leaves, shredded
1 red pepper, seeded and cut into strips	About 2 tbsp harissa (hot chilli sauce)

Heat a small frying pan. Add the cinnamon stick and cloves with the mustard, cumin and coriander seeds. Toast for a couple of minutes until they start to smell aromatic, tossing occasionally. Place the spices in a mini-blender and grind to a powder.

Heat the oil in a large pan. Add the onion and pepper and cook for 2–3 minutes until the onion is softened but not browned. Sprinkle in the spice mixture and cook for another minute or so, stirring. Pour in the stock and add the potatoes and chickpeas. Season to taste, bring to simmer and cook for 15 minutes, or until the potatoes are tender.

Stir in the spinach and enough harissa to taste and cook until the spinach has just wilted. Ladle into bowls, piling up some of the chunky ingredients in the middle of each bowl to serve.

SPICY AUBERGINE AND TOMATO SOUP

This delicious soup has lots of Asian undertones. I like to serve it with minted yoghurt as it tempers the flavours, providing a great contrast.

6 tbsp olive oil	1 tsp each ground cumin and coriander
450g/1lb aubergines, cut into	1 tsp fennel seeds
2cm/¾in slices	Salt and freshly ground black pepper
1 large onion, finely chopped	400g/14oz can chopped tomatoes
2 garlic cloves, finely chopped	900ml/1½ pints vegetable stock
1 red Scotch bonnet chilli, seeded and	400ml/14fl oz coconut milk
finely chopped	Minted yoghurt cooler (page 16), to garnish

Heat 4 tablespoons of the oil in a large frying pan. Add the aubergine slices and cook in batches until lightly golden. Drain on kitchen paper, then roughly chop and set aside.
Heat the remaining oil in a large pan. Add the onion and gently fry for about 10 minutes until slightly caramelized. Add the garlic, chilli and spices and cook for a further 2 minutes. Season generously.
Add the reserved aubergines, the tomatoes, stock and coconut milk and bring to the boil. Reduce the heat and simmer for 20 minutes until slightly reduced and thickened. Season to taste.
Leave to cool a little, then purée in batches in a food processor or with a hand-held liquidizer until smooth. Return to a clean pan and reheat gently. Season to taste and ladle into bowls. Add a good spoonful of the minted yoghurt and serve at once.

CHINESE MUSHROOM SOUP

Dried Chinese mushrooms are readily available in most ethnic shops and oriental stores. Look out for shiitake and wood-ears; I like a combination of both in this soup.

25g/1oz dried Chinese mushrooms	2 tbsp sunflower oil
(see introduction)	1.2 litres/2 pints vegetable or chicken stock
15g/½oz bunch fresh coriander	2 tbsp Thai fish sauce
2.5cm/1in piece root ginger, peeled	50g/2oz vermicelli noodles
and chopped	1 head of pak choi, shredded
2 garlic cloves, chopped	Juice of 1 lime
4 spring onions, sliced on the diagonal,	Good pinch of sugar
white and green parts separated	

Place the mushrooms in a bowl and cover with 150ml/5fl oz hot water. Set aside to soak and swell for 10 minutes, then drain, reserving the soaking liquid, trim away the tough stalks and cut the caps into slices. Chop the coriander, reserving some leaves for garnish. Place the coriander in a mini-blender with the ginger, garlic and the white parts of the spring onions. Whizz to a paste.

Heat the oil in a large pan. Add the coriander paste and stir-fry for 1 minute. Pour in the stock and add the reserved soaking liquid with the mushrooms and fish sauce. Bring to the boil and skim any scum off the surface. Reduce the heat and simmer for 15 minutes until the mushrooms are completely tender.

Place the noodles in a pan of boiling water, remove from the heat and leave to soak for 4 minutes, or according to the packet instructions. Drain and rinse under cold running water. Add the noodles to the soup with the pak choi, lime juice and sugar and heat through until the pak choi has just wilted. Spoon into bowls and garnish with the remaining green spring onions and coriander leaves.

Right: Moroccan Chickpea Soup

ROASTED TOMATO AND CHILLI SOUP

You can pass this soup through a sieve for a smooth texture, but I don't normally bother. If you are not going to sieve the soup, make sure you cut the eye out of each tomato when you halve them, as they are tough and won't break down during cooking.

675g/1¹⁄₂lb plum tomatoes, halved
Sea salt and freshly ground black pepper
2 mild red chillies, halved and seeded
1 large garlic clove, halved
12 large basil leaves
4 tbsp extra virgin olive oil, plus extra to garnish

900ml/1¹⁄₂ pints chicken or vegetable stock
300g/10oz olive oil bread, such as ciabatta, crusts removed
Pared Parmesan shavings, to serve

Preheat the oven to 200°C/400°F/Gas 6. Put the tomatoes in a roasting tin, cut side up, and season generously. Add the chillies, garlic and 6 of the basil leaves. Drizzle over half of the oil and roast for 20–25 minutes until the tomatoes are softened and lightly charred around the edges.

Tip the tomato mixture into a food processor and whizz until just blended. Pass through a sieve, if liked, and place in a large pan. Pour in the stock, season to taste and simmer for 5 minutes until well mixed and thickened.

Break the bread into small chunks and stir into the soup until the bread has softened and is well mixed with the tomatoes. Tear the remaining basil leaves into small pieces and stir into the soup. Ladle into bowls, garnish with Parmesan shavings and a drizzle of oil and serve at once.

MULLIGATAWNY SOUP

Here's a simple version of a classic curried soup. You could also omit the cream and leave the soup chunky for a more substantial meal.

50g/2oz unsalted butter
1 large onion, finely chopped
1 heaped tbsp good-quality medium curry paste
2 carrots, diced
1 parsnip, diced
1 potato, diced

100g/4oz chestnut mushrooms, diced
900ml/1¹⁄₂ pints vegetable stock
150ml/5fl oz double cream
2 tbsp chopped fresh coriander
Juice of ¹⁄₂ lemon
Salt and freshly ground black pepper
1 dessert apple, peeled, cored and diced

Melt the butter in a large pan. Add most of the onion, reserving a little for a garnish, and cook gently for about 10 minutes until lightly caramelized. Stir in the curry paste and cook for another minute or so, stirring. Add the vegetables and cook for another 2–3 minutes, then pour in the stock and bring to the boil. Reduce the heat and simmer for 30 minutes, or until the vegetables are completely tender.

Leave to cool a little, then purée in batches in a food processor or with a hand-held liquidizer until smooth. Return to a clean pan, adding a little water if the soup needs thinning down. Add the cream and coriander and reheat gently. Add a little of the lemon juice, season to taste and ladle into bowls. Mix the reserved onion with the apple and the remaining lemon juice and sprinkle over the soup to serve.

HOT AND SOUR PRAWN SOUP

This spicy oriental soup will certainly revive your senses at the end of the day. How hot you make it is up to you – birds' eye chillies are very fiery indeed, so reduce the quantity if you are unsure.

1 tbsp chilli oil
450g/1lb raw tiger prawns, peeled and de-veined, with shells reserved
900ml/1¹⁄₂ pints chicken stock
2 lemon grass stalks, roughly chopped
4 kaffir lime leaves
3 red birds' eye chillies, finely chopped

1 star anise
Juice of 2 lemons
6 tbsp Thai fish sauce
1 tsp sugar
225g/8oz can straw mushrooms, drained and rinsed
Fresh coriander leaves, to garnish

Heat the oil in a large pan. Add the prawn shells and sauté until the shells have turned bright pink. Pour in the stock, add the lemon grass, lime leaves, chillies and star anise and bring to the boil. Reduce the heat and simmer for 15 minutes to allow the flavours to infuse. Strain through a fine sieve into a clean pan.

Add the lemon juice, fish sauce and sugar and simmer for a further 2 minutes. Add the prawns and mushrooms, stir and cook for a further 2–3 minutes until the prawns are cooked through. Ladle into soup bowls and serve at once.

TURKEY WONTON LAKSA

In Malaysia, *laksa* is the name of a creamy coconut rice noodle dish. This variation was made up to use the left-over turkey at Christmas.

1 tbsp sunflower oil
2 heaped tsp freshly grated root ginger
2 garlic cloves, finely chopped
1 tsp each ground turmeric and coriander
2 heaped tbsp Thai red curry paste
600ml/1 pint chicken stock
400ml/14fl oz coconut milk
150g/5oz cooked turkey, finely chopped

Good dash light soy sauce
1 tsp sesame oil
4 tbsp roughly chopped fresh coriander
18 wonton wrappers
175g/6oz rice vermicelli noodles
Juice of 1 lime
4 spring onions, finely sliced

Heat the oil in a large pan. Add half of the ginger and garlic, the turmeric, ground coriander and curry paste and cook for a minute or so, stirring. Pour in the stock and coconut milk and bring to the boil. Reduce the heat and simmer gently for 8–10 minutes.

Place the turkey in a bowl with the remaining ginger and garlic, the soy sauce and sesame oil. Add half of the fresh coriander and stir to mix. Place 1 heaped teaspoon into each wonton wrapper, brush the edges with a little water and bring them up to form a triangular parcel, pressing the edges together to seal. Arrange the wontons in a steamer set over the pan of soup and steam for 4–5 minutes until transparent.

Place the noodles in a pan of boiling water, remove from the heat and set aside for 3–4 minutes, or according to the packet instructions. Drain and place some in each serving bowl. Stir the lime juice into the soup. Ladle over the noodles and arrange the wontons on top. Scatter over the remaining coriander and spring onions to serve.

Right: Roasted Tomato and Chilli Soup

ENTERTAINING

Entertaining, whatever the occasion, can take hours of preparation, yet the results can be devoured by your guests in a matter of moments. The great thing about the soups in this chapter is that you can make all of them in advance and keep them chilled in the fridge (and most can be frozen), ready for every eventuality. All recipes serve 4–6.

CRAB BISQUE

This is an extremely rich soup so serve it in small amounts if you want your guests to have any room left for other courses! You can substitute lobster for the crab for an even more decadent flavour.

675g/1½lb cooked crab
100g/4oz unsalted butter
100g/4oz each onion, carrot, leek, celery and fennel, diced
1 fresh bouquet garni
4 ripe tomatoes, quartered

4 tbsp brandy (Cognac if possible)
2 tsp tomato purée
150ml/5fl oz dry white wine
900ml/1½ pints fish stock
Salt and freshly ground black pepper
Tarragon herb cream, to serve (page 16)

Remove the white and brown crab meat from the legs, back shell and body, discarding the dead man's fingers. Place pieces of the shell in a polythene bag and smash into small pieces.

Melt half the butter in a large pan. Add the diced vegetables, stirring to coat them in the butter, then add the crushed crab shell and bouquet garni, stir well, cover and cook for 10–15 minutes until the vegetables are softened but not coloured.

Add the tomatoes to the pan and cook for another 5 minutes, then increase the heat and pour in the brandy – it should boil down and reduce immediately. Add the tomato purée, wine and stock and bring to a simmer, then continue to simmer for 30 minutes until well flavoured and slightly reduced. Season to taste.

Press the crab-shell mixture through a fine sieve, pressing out as much liquid as possible with the back of a ladle or a wooden spoon. Ladle the sieved liquid into a food processor and add the remaining butter and the most of the crab meat, reserving some of the white meat to garnish. Whizz until blended.

Return the soup to a clean pan and season to taste. Reheat gently, then ladle into bowls, add a sprinkling of the reserved crab meat and a spoonful of the tarragon herb cream to serve.

BOUILLABAISSE

This soup is renowned the world over and for a very good reason. It uses a whole selection of Mediterranean fish and shellfish to produce a very intense, saffron-flavoured broth, which is served separately from the fish and potatoes.

900g/2lb prepared mixed fish and shellfish, such as small pieces of red mullet, sea bass, John Dory or monkfish fillets and clams, mussels and whole prawns
2 large onions, halved and thinly sliced
2 large garlic cloves, crushed
1 celery stick, diced
350g/12oz waxy potatoes, thickly sliced and rinsed
225g/8oz ripe tomatoes, peeled and chopped

Thinly shredded rind of ½ orange
1 bay leaf
1 sprig each fresh thyme and fennel
2 whole cloves
Few black peppercorns
175ml/6fl oz olive oil
Sea salt
1.7 litres/2½ pints boiling water
Few saffron strands soaked in 1 tbsp hot water
Rouille and Croûtes (pages 12 and 14), to serve

Discard any cracked or open clams or mussels that do not close when tapped. Place the onions, garlic, celery, potatoes and tomatoes in a large pan with the orange rind, herbs and spices. Pour over half of the olive oil and season generously with salt. Pour in the water and bring to the boil. Reduce the heat, cover and simmer for 10 minutes.

Arrange the fish on top and pour over the remaining oil and the saffron. Return to the boil and cover. Reduce the heat and simmer for another 8 minutes. Add the shellfish, cover again and continue to simmer for another 5 minutes, or until the shellfish have just opened and the fish are still holding their shape. Discard any mussels and clams that are not open.

Carefully remove the fish and shellfish from the pan and arrange on a large platter with the potatoes. Ladle the broth into bowls and serve both at the same time with the rouille and croûtes in separate bowls.

SAFFRON MUSSEL SOUP

This has to be one of the finest dishes I have ever eaten.
Don't overcook the leeks or they will lose their vibrant green colour.

2kg/4½lb fresh mussels, cleaned
300ml/10fl oz dry white wine
1 tsp medium curry powder
1 tsp sugar
2 garlic cloves, peeled
Good pinch saffron strands,
soaked in 1 tbsp hot water

25g/1oz unsalted butter
2 large shallots, finely chopped
2 leeks, sliced
750ml/1¼ pints fish stock
150ml/5fl oz double cream
2 tbsp snipped fresh chives
Salt and freshly ground black pepper

Discard any cracked or open mussels that do not close when tapped.
Place the wine, curry powder, sugar and garlic in a large pan and season
with pepper. Bring to the boil, then add the saffron. Add the mussels,
cover and cook over a high heat for 3–5 minutes, shaking the pan
occasionally, until they have all opened. Drain the mussels, reserving
the cooking liquid and discarding the garlic and any mussels that have
not opened. When the mussels are cool enough to handle, remove
most of them from their shells, reserving a few whole ones for garnish.

Melt the butter in the pan. Add the shallots and cook for about
5 minutes until softened but not browned, stirring occasionally.
Add the leeks and cook for another few minutes until softened but still
holding their colour. Pour in the stock and strain in the reserved mussel
cooking liquid through a piece of double muslin to remove any sand
and grit, then bring to a simmer. Add the mussels, cream and chives
and just heat through, without boiling. Season to taste, ladle into bowls
and garnish with the reserved whole mussels to serve.

WILD MUSHROOM SOUP

Soup made from wild mushrooms has the most extraordinary, intense
flavour. I find they make the best soup when they are a few days old
and have darkened a bit.

25g/1oz dried cep mushrooms
50g/2oz unsalted butter
1 onion, finely chopped
1 garlic clove, crushed
450g/1lb wild mushrooms, sliced

600ml/1 pint chicken stock
2 slices white bread, crusts removed
Salt and freshly ground black pepper
150ml/5fl oz single cream
Parmesan croûtons (page 14), to serve

Soak the dried ceps in 150ml/5fl oz boiling water for 15 minutes.
Drain, reserving the soaking liquid. Finely chop the ceps and set aside.

Melt the butter in a large pan. Add the onion and garlic and cook for
10 minutes until softened but not coloured. Increase the heat, add the
fresh mushrooms and stir-fry for 3–4 minutes until just tender. Pour in
the chicken stock and reserved mushroom soaking liquid, add the
reconstituted ceps and bring to the boil. Reduce the heat and simmer
for 15–20 minutes until the mushrooms are completely tender and the
liquid has slightly reduced.

Crumble the bread into the soup and season to taste. Purée in batches
in a food processor or with a hand-held liquidizer. Pour back into the
clean pan, season to taste and add the cream. Reheat gently without
boiling, then ladle into bowls and garnish with Parmesan croûtons.
Serve at once.

ARTICHOKE AND SMOKED BACON SOUP

When you prepare the artichokes, place them immediately in a bowl of
water with a good squeeze of lemon juice to stop them turning brown.
You can fry extra bacon and reserve to use as a garnish with swirls of
unwhipped cream, instead of the blue cheese butter, if you wish.

2 tbsp sunflower oil
100g/4oz smoked bacon lardons
25g/1oz unsalted butter
1 large onion, finely chopped
675g/1½lb Jerusalem artichokes,
peeled and thinly sliced

900ml/1½ pints vegetable stock
Salt and freshly ground black pepper
Thin slices of Blue cheese butter
(page 16), to garnish

Heat the oil in a large pan. Add the bacon lardons and cook for about
5 minutes, stirring occasionally until crisp. Add the butter and then add
the onion, stirring to coat. Reduce the heat and cook gently for 8–10
minutes until the onion has softened but not coloured.

Drain the artichokes (see above) and add to the pan with the stock.
Season to taste and bring to the boil. Reduce the heat and simmer
gently for about 30 minutes until the artichokes are completely tender.

Purée the soup in batches in a food processor or with a hand-held
liquidizer. Pour back into a clean pan, season to taste and reheat gently.
Ladle into bowls and garnish with thin slices of the blue cheese butter.

Right: Saffron Mussel Soup

WATERCRESS AND POTATO SOUP

You can also serve this chilled, garnished with crumbled Roquefort cheese for a special treat. Roasting the garlic gives the soup an underlying smoky taste, which is sublime.

4 large garlic cloves, unpeeled
2 tbsp olive oil
25g/1oz unsalted butter
1 onion, finely chopped
2 bunches fresh watercress

225g/8oz potatoes, diced
900ml/1½ pints chicken or
vegetable stock
Salt and freshly ground black pepper
2 egg yolks

Preheat the oven to 200°C/400°F/Gas 6. Place the garlic in a very small roasting tin, drizzle over half of the oil and roast for 25–30 minutes until completely tender and lightly charred. Leave until cool enough to handle, then slip the flesh out of the skins and reserve.

Heat the remaining oil with the butter in a pan. Add the onion and cook for 2–3 minutes until softened but not browned. Chop up the watercress, separating the leaves and stalks. Add the watercress stalks to the onion with the potatoes, cover and cook gently for 10 minutes until the potatoes are nearly tender but not browned, stirring occasionally.

Pour in the stock, season to taste and bring to the boil. Reduce the heat and simmer for 20 minutes until the potatoes are completely soft and the soup has thickened slightly. Add the roasted garlic with the reserved watercress leaves, keeping some back to garnish, and simmer for 1 minute, then remove from the heat.

Leave the soup to cool a little, then purée in batches in a food processor or with a hand-held liquidizer. Pour back into a clean pan, season to taste and reheat gently. Beat together the egg yolks and cream and stir a ladleful of the soup into the mixture. Stir the mixture into the soup and just warm through, without boiling. Ladle into bowls and garnish with the reserved watercress leaves to serve.

ROYAL SALMON SOUP

I love all fish soups, but this one has a wonderful rich flavour that is hard to beat, especially when it is served with garlic croûtes spread with rouille. For a smoother, more velvety finish pass the soup through a fine sieve.

40g/1½oz unsalted butter
1 large onion, chopped
2 carrots, chopped
2 celery sticks, chopped
1 small fennel bulb, chopped
4 plum tomatoes, peeled,
seeded and chopped
2 heaped tbsp each chopped fresh
basil and tarragon
Pinch of saffron strands,
soaked in 1 tbsp hot water

300ml/10fl oz dry white wine
900ml/1½ pints fish stock
1 tsp tomato purée
300g/10oz salmon fillets,
skinned and chopped
Salt and freshly ground black pepper
Garlic croûtes with Rouille
(pages 14 and 12)

Melt the butter in a large pan. Add the onion, carrots, celery, fennel and tomatoes and cook gently for about 5 minutes, stirring until almost tender but not coloured. Stir in the herbs and saffron and cook for another 1–2 minutes, then pour in the white wine and allow to reduce a little. Add the fish stock and tomato purée and simmer for 10–15 minutes until all the flavours are well combined and the vegetables are completely tender.

Stir the salmon into the soup and simmer for another 5 minutes or so until the salmon is just tender and cooked through. Season to taste. Purée the soup in batches in a food processor or with a hand-held liquidizer and push through a fine sieve, if liked (see introduction). Pour back into a clean pan and season to taste. Reheat gently, then ladle into bowls and serve at once with the rouille-topped croûtes.

Right: *Watercress and Potato Soup*

TOMATO SOUP WITH FISH QUENELLES

As the fish quenelles are made from a mousse-like mixture it is very important to keep the mixture as cold as possible at all times so you achieve a light and fluffy result.

*225g/8oz sole or plaice fillets, skinned,
chopped and chilled
1 egg white, chilled
Grated rind of 1 lemon
1 tbsp snipped fresh chives
Salt and freshly ground black pepper
120ml/4fl oz double cream, chilled
2 tbsp olive oil*

*1 onion, finely chopped
2 garlic cloves, finely chopped
1 small fennel bulb, finely chopped
with fronds reserved
225g/8oz ripe tomatoes,
peeled and chopped
150ml/5fl oz dry white wine
900ml/1½ pints fish stock*

To make the quenelles, place the fish in a food processor and whizz until finely minced. With the motor running, slowly pour in the egg white and blend until just combined. Transfer to a bowl, cover with clingfilm and chill for 30 minutes. Stir in the lemon rind and chives and season to taste. Gradually beat in the cream, a little at a time, until combined. Cover with clingfilm and chill for 30 minutes.

Heat the oil in a large pan. Add the onion and garlic and cook for 5 minutes until softened. Add the fennel and cook for 5 minutes, stirring occasionally. Add the tomatoes and wine and continue to cook for 10 minutes until reduced and thickened. Pour in the stock, season to taste and bring to the boil. Reduce the heat and simmer for 15 minutes until the fennel is tender and the soup has thickened slightly.

Leave to cool a little, then purée in batches in a food processor or with a hand-held liquidizer. Season and pass through a sieve back into a clean pan.

To cook the quenelles, shape the fish mixture into 12–18 quenelles with two dessertspoons and place straight into a pan of simmering salted water. Cook for 1 minute, or until they rise to the top. Drain on kitchen paper.

Reheat the soup and ladle into bowls. Arrange 3 quenelles in each bowl and garnish with the fennel fronds.

VICHYSSOISE

This is a classic soup which was invented by a Frenchman living in America. It is always served chilled and has provided the inspiration for many, many variations by world famous chefs.

*50g/2oz unsalted butter
350g/12oz small leeks, finely chopped
1 onion, finely chopped
225g/8oz potatoes, diced
1 celery stick, diced
1 garlic clove, crushed*

*Salt and freshly ground pepper
900ml/1½ pints chicken stock
150ml/5fl oz milk
150ml/5fl oz double cream
Snipped fresh chives, to garnish*

Melt the butter in a large heavy-based pan. As soon as it foams, stir in the leeks, onion, potatoes and celery until well coated. Add the garlic and season generously, then press a circle of buttered parchment paper on top of the vegetables. Cover the pan with a tight-fitting lid and cook gently on a low heat for about 10 minutes, shaking the pan occasionally, until the vegetables are soft but just beginning to colour.

Remove the lid and the paper from the pan, pour in the stock and bring to the boil. Reduce the heat and simmer for about 5 minutes until the potatoes are completely tender. Purée the soup in batches in a food processor or with a hand-held liquidizer.

Push the puréed soup through a fine sieve into a large bowl. Season to taste and stir in the milk and most of the cream, reserving some for garnish. Cover with clingfilm and chill for at least 2 hours, but overnight is best. To serve, ladle into bowls and swirl in the reserved cream. Garnish with the chives and serve ice cold.

CHILLED MELON SOUP

What could be more refreshing than a bowl of icy melon soup on a hot summer's day? For a really special treat, replace the melons below with six small ones. Cut a 2.5cm/1in slice off the top of each one and hollow them out so you can use the shells as bowls in which to serve the soup. Prop the lids alongside.

*3 ripe charentais or cantaloupe melons
6 spring onions, finely chopped
4 tbsp elderflower cordial
1 heaped tbsp chopped fresh dill,
plus extra sprigs to garnish*

*200ml/7fl oz crème fraîche
About 450ml/15fl oz still mineral water
Salt and freshly ground black pepper
Lime-infused yoghurt (page 16), to serve*

Cut each melon in half and discard the seeds, then scoop out the flesh and roughly chop, reserving the juices. Place the melon flesh in a food processor with the spring onions, elderflower cordial, dill and crème fraîche. Blend to a purée and transfer to a bowl. Stir in any reserved juice and enough of the water to give the required consistency. Season to taste.

Cover the soup with clingfilm and chill for at least 2 hours, but overnight is best. To serve, stir the soup well, then ladle into bowls, add spoonfuls of the lime-infused yoghurt and garnish with dill sprigs.

Right: Tomato Soup with Fish Quenelles

PRAWN AND FENNEL SOUP

This soup has a surprisingly delicate flavour with subtle aniseed tones. If you are lucky enough to get hold of whole prawns, peel them and then bash the shells with a rolling pin. Place the shells in a pan with the fish stock and simmer for about 20 minutes, then strain before using for a much more intensely flavoured stock.

50g/2oz unsalted butter
2 large fennel bulbs, finely chopped
with fronds reserved
4 large shallots, finely chopped
4 tbsp Pernod

150ml/5fl oz dry white wine
Salt and freshly ground black pepper
900ml/1½ pints fish stock
450g/1lb shelled raw prawns, de-veined
150ml/5fl oz double cream

Melt the butter in a large pan. Add the fennel and shallots and cook gently for 20–30 minutes, stirring occasionally until the vegetables are completely softened and beginning to caramelize. Add the Pernod and allow to bubble away completely, stirring constantly, then pour in the wine and simmer gently for about 5 minutes until reduced by half. Season to taste.

Pour in the stock and bring to the boil. Reduce the heat and simmer for 15–20 minutes until the flavours are well combined and the liquid has reduced slightly. Purée the soup in batches in a food processor or with a hand-held liquidizer.

Push the puréed soup through a fine sieve back into a clean pan and stir in the prawns and cream. Season to taste and reheat gently for 2–3 minutes without boiling until the prawns have turned pink and opaque, then ladle into bowls. Add a good grinding of black pepper and sprinkle the reserved fennel fronds on top. Serve at once.

SWEET POTATO AND COCONUT SOUP

This soup has both Thai and Caribbean influences, and tastes out of this world. It has to be one of my all-time favourites.

50g/2oz unsalted butter
4 large shallots, finely chopped
450g/1lb sweet potatoes, peeled and diced
2 red birds' eye chillies, seeded
and finely chopped
15g/½oz bunch fresh coriander,
stalks and leaves separated and both
finely chopped

225g/8oz ripe plum tomatoes, peeled,
seeded and diced
900ml/1½ pints chicken stock
400ml/14fl oz coconut milk
Salt and freshly ground black pepper
Crispy seaweed (page 15), to garnish

Melt the butter in a large heavy-based pan. Add the shallots and cook for 2–3 minutes until just beginning to soften. Stir in the sweet potatoes until well coated. Press a circle of buttered parchment paper on top of the vegetables. Cover the pan with a tight-fitting lid and cook gently on a low heat for about 10 minutes, shaking the pan occasionally, until the sweet potatoes have softened but not coloured.

Remove the lid and the paper and stir in the chillies, coriander stalks and tomatoes then cook for another 1–2 minutes, stirring. Pour in the stock and coconut milk and bring to the boil. Reduce the heat and simmer for another 20–25 minutes until the sweet potatoes are completely tender and the liquid has slightly reduced.

Stir the coriander leaves into the soup and then purée in batches in a food processor or with a hand-held liquidizer. Pour back into the pan, season to taste and reheat gently. Ladle into bowls and pile small mounds of the crispy seaweed into the centre of each to serve.

ASPARAGUS AND MASCARPONE TORTE SOUP

Mascarpone torte, with its layers of mascarpone and gorgonzola, is seductively rich and delicate, making it a perfect partner for asparagus.

675g/1¹/₂lb asparagus,
woody ends removed
50g/2oz unsalted butter
2 large shallots, finely chopped
1 potato, diced

900ml/1¹/₂ pints chicken or vegetable stock
Salt and freshly ground black pepper
175g/6oz mascarpone torte cheese,
crumbled
4 tbsp single cream

Cut the top 5cm/2in off the asparagus stalks and simmer them gently in boiling water for 3–4 minutes until just tender. Drain well, refresh under cold running water and set aside. Slice the remaining stalks.

Melt the butter in a large pan. Add the shallots, potato and sliced asparagus stalks, cover and cook gently for 10 minutes until softened but not coloured, stirring once or twice. Pour in the stock, season to taste and bring the boil. Reduce the heat and simmer for 20 minutes until the potatoes are tender and the soup has thickened slightly.

Purée the soup in batches in a food processor or with a hand-held liquidizer. Return to the pan and whisk in most of the cheese, reserving some for a garnish. Season to taste and reheat gently, being careful not to boil. Serve hot or chilled; ladle into bowls, top with a swirl of the cream and garnish with the reserved asparagus tips and crumbled mascarpone torte.

Above: Asparagus and Mascarpone Torte Soup

CREAM OF CELERIAC SOUP

Celeriac is an unusual looking root vegetable with a subtle, celery-like flavour. Choose your specimen carefully: if you buy a particularly knobbly one there can be a lot of wastage once it has been peeled.

50g/2oz unsalted butter
675g/1¹/₂lb whole celeriac bulb,
peeled and diced
1 large onion, finely chopped
900ml/1¹/₂ pints vegetable stock

4 tbsp single cream
Squeeze of lemon juice
Salt and freshly ground black pepper
Dill herb cream (page 16), to serve

Melt the butter in a large pan. Add the celeriac and onion and cook gently for 1–2 minutes, stirring constantly. Press a buttered circle of parchment paper on to the vegetables and cover with a tight-fitting lid. Cook gently for about 10 minutes, shaking the pan occasionally, until the vegetables are softened and have just started to colour.

Remove the lid and paper, pour in the stock and bring to the boil. Reduce the heat and simmer for 25–30 minutes until the celeriac is completely tender and the liquid has reduced slightly. Purée in batches in a food processor or with a hand-held liquidizer.

Push the puréed soup through a fine sieve back into a clean pan and stir in the cream and lemon juice. Season to taste and reheat gently until just warmed through. Ladle into bowls and add a good spoonful of the dill herb cream. Serve at once.

WHITE GARLIC GAZPACHO

This is a popular Spanish soup with a delicate but pungent flavour. It should be served well chilled and in small portions; it will definitely serve six.

85g/3oz blanched almonds
4 large garlic cloves, chopped
100g/4oz unbleached white bread,
crusts removed
About 600ml/1 pint still mineral water
120ml/4fl oz extra virgin olive oil,
plus extra to garnish

1 tbsp sherry vinegar
1 tsp salt
350g/12oz Muscat grapes, peeled,
halved and pips removed
6 ice cubes
Paprika, for dusting

Place the almonds, garlic and bread in a food processor and whizz to a paste, adding a little of the water if necessary to move the mixture around. Gradually add the oil, vinegar and enough of the remaining water to make a smooth soup. Season to taste with salt.

Pour into a bowl and cover tightly with clingfilm. Chill for at least 2 hours, but overnight is best. Remove from the fridge, give a good stir and correct the seasoning and adjust the consistency as necessary with a little more water. Fold in the grapes. Ladle into small colourful bowls and add an ice cube and a drizzle of the olive oil to each portion. Sprinkle over a little paprika and serve ice cold.

LIGHT & HEALTHY

When you come home late after work or an evening out, a full-scale dinner is often out of the question, but a light and wholesome bowl of soup can just fit the bill. These are recipes low on fat and high on flavour. You will find that a diet that revolves around soup is not only a healthy diet, but also can be a perfect solution for anyone who wants to lose weight. All recipes serve 4–6.

CARROT AND GINGER SOUP

This is not only cheap and easy to make, but it has a fantastic vibrant colour. What more do you want?

1 tbsp sunflower oil	1 tbsp clear honey
1 large onion, finely chopped	Squeeze of lemon juice
2 tbsp freshly grated root ginger	Salt and freshly ground black pepper
675g/1½ lb carrots, grated	

Heat the oil in a large pan. Add the onion and ginger and cook over a low heat for 10 minutes until completely softened but not browned.

Stir in the carrots, honey and lemon juice, pour in 900ml/1½ pints water and bring to the boil. Reduce the heat and simmer for 40 minutes, or until the carrots are soft and the soup has thickened.

Purée the soup in batches in a food processor or with a hand-held liquidizer. To serve, reheat gently and season to taste. Ladle into bowls and add a grinding of black pepper to serve.

RED PEPPER AND TOMATO SOUP

Lovely to eat at any time of the year, this soup is, however, best at the end of the summer when tomatoes are plentiful and cheap. If you can't find any decent ones replace the quantity below with a 400g/14oz can chopped tomatoes (in rich tomato juice) or 450ml/15fl oz passata (sieved tomatoes).

1 tbsp olive oil	2 large red peppers, seeded and chopped
6 spring onions, finely chopped, with	Salt and freshly ground black pepper
white and green parts separated	900ml/1½ pints vegetable or chicken stock
450g/1lb ripe tomatoes, peeled,	Pinch of sugar
seeded and chopped	4–6 tbsp low-fat fromage frais

Heat the olive oil in a large pan. Add the white parts of the spring onions and cook for a minute or so. Add the tomatoes and peppers and cook for another 5 minutes, or until tender. Season generously, pour in the stock and bring to the boil. Reduce the heat and simmer for 10 minutes until reduced and thickened slightly.

Purée in batches in a food processor or with a hand-held liquidizer. Pour back into a clean pan and stir in the green part of the spring onions and the sugar. Season to taste and reheat gently. Ladle into bowls and garnish with a spoonful of the fromage frais. Add a good grinding of black pepper to serve.

CUCUMBER AND YOGHURT SOUP

This refreshing and delicious combination is great for hot days or as a soup course during a spicy meal to help clean the palate.

2 cucumbers, peeled, seeded and chopped	8 drops of Tabasco
1 tsp fine sea salt	2 heaped tbsp chopped mixed fresh chives,
300ml/10fl oz chicken stock	dill, mint, tarragon and flat-leaf parsley
600ml/1 pint Greek strained yoghurt	Salt and freshly ground black pepper
150ml/5fl oz soured cream	Salsa fresca (page 12), to serve

Place the cucumber in a colander, sprinkle over the salt and set aside for 30 minutes, then rinse well under cold running water and squeeze out the excess moisture in a clean tea towel.

Place the cucumber in a food processor with the stock, yoghurt, soured cream, Tabasco, herbs and plenty of seasoning and blend to a purée – you may have to do this in batches. Pour into a large bowl and cover with clingfilm. Chill for at least 2 hours, but overnight is best.

Remove the soup from the fridge and give it a good stir. Season to taste and ladle into bowls. Scatter over some salsa fresca and serve ice cold.

SPICY WINTER VEGETABLE SOUP

You can substitute pumpkin, swede or turnip for the parsnips and carrots, or just use a mixture – this is a very flexible recipe.

1 tbsp olive oil	1 tbsp medium curry powder or paste
2 small leeks, thinly sliced	900ml/1½ pints vegetable stock
350g/12oz parsnips, diced	Salt and freshly ground black pepper
225g/8oz carrots, diced	150ml/5fl oz semi-skimmed milk
100g/4oz potato, diced	Toasted cumin seeds, to garnish

Heat the oil in a large pan. Add the vegetables and cook for a minute or so until well coated. Reduce the heat, cover and cook for about 10 minutes, stirring occasionally until softened but not coloured. Stir in the curry powder or paste and cook for another minute or so, stirring.

Pour in the stock, season to taste and bring to the boil. Reduce the heat and simmer for 25–30 minutes until the vegetables are completely tender and the liquid has reduced slightly.

Allow the soup to cool a little, then purée in batches in a food processor or with a hand-held liquidizer. Return to a clean pan and stir in the milk. Reheat gently until just warmed through, without boiling. Ladle into bowls and garnish with toasted cumin seeds. Serve at once.

BEETROOT BORSCHT

'Borscht' or 'borshch' is a general name for a number of Eastern European beetroot soups that vary a great deal – however, this version is my favourite.

1 tbsp olive oil
1 large leek, finely chopped
2 celery sticks, finely chopped
450g/1lb raw beetroot, peeled and finely grated
1 potato, diced
200g/7oz carrot, finely grated

900ml/1½ pints vegetable or chicken stock
1 tbsp red wine vinegar
1 tsp sugar
Salt and freshly ground black pepper
About 2 tbsp soured cream (optional)

Heat the oil in a large pan. Add the leek and celery and fry for about 5 minutes until softened. Add the beetroot, potato and most of the carrot, reserving some for garnish. Pour in the stock and bring to the boil. Reduce the heat and simmer for 40 minutes, or until the vegetables are completely tender and the soup has thickened slightly.

Stir in the vinegar and sugar and season to taste. To serve, ladle into bowls and garnish with a small spoonful of soured cream, if using, and a little grated carrot.

Above: Beetroot Borscht

OYSTER AND LEEK SOUP

This is a special soup with a spicy kick that has fresh oysters added at the last minute. It is the perfect starter for a romantic meal.

1 tbsp olive oil
4 large shallots, finely chopped
1 mild red chilli, seeded and finely chopped
900ml/1½ pints fish stock
4 small leeks, thinly sliced

2 dozen oysters, opened and loosened (with juices reserved)
1 heaped tsp chopped fresh chervil
Salt and freshly ground black pepper
½ lemon, pips removed

Heat the oil in a large pan. Add the shallots and chilli and cook gently for about 5 minutes until softened. Pour in the stock and bring to the boil. Reduce the heat and simmer for 5 minutes, or until the flavours are well combined.

Add the leeks and simmer for another 2 minutes until they are just tender and still bright green. Add the oysters and strain in their juice through a fine sieve to remove any of the little pieces of shell. Stir in the chervil and season to taste. Bring to a gentle simmer to just barely poach the oysters and remove from the heat. Add a squeeze of lemon juice to taste.

Divide the oysters between serving bowls and ladle over the remaining broth. Serve at once with a glass of chilled Champagne. Enjoy!

SPRING PEA SOUP

You don't have to use fresh peas for this soup, as frozen work just as well, but the flavours are all colourful and vibrant, hence the name.

450g/1lb shelled fresh or frozen peas
Juice of 1 lime
2 heaped tbsp fresh basil leaves, plus extra to garnish
2 mild red chillies, seeded and finely chopped
½ tsp ground cumin
½ tsp ground coriander
Good pinch paprika, plus extra to garnish

Salt and freshly ground black pepper
1 tbsp olive oil
6 spring onions, finely chopped
1 garlic clove, crushed
900ml/1½ pints vegetable stock
2 ripe plum tomatoes, peeled, seeded and diced
Lime-infused yoghurt (page 16), to garnish (optional)

Place the peas in a pan of boiling salted water and cook for 4–5 minutes until just tender. Drain and refresh under cold running water.

Place the lime juice in a food processor with the fresh basil and chillies and blend until smooth. Add the peas with the ground cumin and coriander, the paprika and plenty of seasoning and blend again until smooth.

Heat the oil in a large pan. Add the spring onions and garlic and cook for 1–2 minutes, stirring. Add the pea mixture and then gradually pour in the stock, stirring to combine. Stir in the tomatoes, bring to a simmer and just heat through.

Season to taste and remove the soup from the heat. Ladle into bowls and add a spoonful of the lime-infused yoghurt, if liked. Garnish with a sprinkling of paprika and some torn basil leaves. Serve at once.

WATERCRESS AND APPLE SOUP

The natural sweetness of the apples gives this soup a wonderful flavour.
It can be served either warm or ice cold, depending on the season.

1 tbsp olive oil
2 leeks, thinly sliced
2 bunches fresh watercress
3 dessert apples, peeled, cored and diced
½ lemon, pips removed

100g/4oz potato, peeled and diced
900ml/1½ pints chicken or
vegetable stock
Salt and freshly ground black pepper
150g/5oz Greek strained yoghurt

Heat the oil in a pan. Add the leeks and cook for about 5 minutes until
softened but not browned. Chop the watercress, separating the leaves
and stalks. Add the watercress stalks to the leeks with most of the
apples, reserving some for garnish with a squeeze of the lemon juice
to them to stop them turning brown. Add the potato to the pan, cover
and cook gently for 10 minutes until the potato is just tender but not
browned, stirring occasionally.

Pour in the stock, season to taste and bring to the boil. Reduce the heat
and simmer for 20 minutes until the apples and potato are completely
soft and the soup has thickened slightly. Add the reserved watercress
leaves, keeping some back for garnish and simmer for 1 minute, then
remove from the heat.

Purée the soup in batches in a food processor or with a hand-held
liquidizer. Pour back into a clean pan and whisk in the yoghurt, then
season to taste and add the remaining lemon juice to taste. Reheat
gently to warm through, then ladle into bowls and garnish with the
reserved diced apple and watercress leaves. Serve at once.

SORREL SOUP

Sorrel is a soft, leafy green herb that has a sharp, almost lemon flavour.
It is now available in most major supermarkets and keeps very well in a
polythene bag in the salad drawer of the fridge. However, if you have
any problems finding it, use tender young spinach leaves instead.

1 tbsp olive oil
1 onion, finely chopped
1 large garlic clove, crushed
1 bay leaf
225g/8oz potato, peeled and diced

2 celery sticks, diced
900ml/1½ pints vegetable stock
50g/2oz sorrel leaves
Salt and freshly ground black pepper

Heat the oil in a large pan. Add the onion, garlic and bay leaf and cook
for about 5 minutes until softened but not coloured. Add the potato
and celery and cook for another 1–2 minutes, stirring.

Pour in the stock and bring to the boil. Reduce the heat and simmer
for 15–20 minutes until the vegetables are completely tender.

Add the sorrel and cook for another minute, stirring constantly.
Remove the bay leaf and purée in batches in a food processor or with
a hand-held liquidizer. Pour back into a clean pan, season to taste and
reheat gently. Ladle into bowls and add a good grinding of black pepper
to serve.

Above: *Quick Gazpacho*

QUICK GAZPACHO

It is worth remembering when making this soup that cold food needs
to be highly seasoned to bring out the best flavours.

900ml/1½ pints tomato juice
1 red pepper, seeded and chopped
1 red onion, seeded and chopped
1 small cucumber, peeled,
seeded and chopped
1 garlic clove, chopped

Handful fresh basil leaves,
plus extra to garnish
1 tbsp extra virgin olive oil
1 tbsp red wine vinegar
1 tsp sugar
Salt and freshly ground black pepper

Place the tomato juice, red pepper, onion, cucumber, garlic, basil, olive
oil, vinegar and sugar in a food processor and blend to a smooth purée
– you may have to do this in batches. Season to taste and chill until
very cold. To serve, ladle into bowls and shred the remaining basil
leaves on top to garnish.

GREEN SUMMER SOUP

This is fabulous on a hot summer's day. If your diet allows, garnish each serving with a frozen olive-oil cube, made in an ice-cube tray.

1 small cucumber, peeled, seeded and finely chopped	1 small garlic clove, crushed
Salt and freshly ground black pepper	450ml/15fl oz vegetable stock
300ml/10fl oz natural yoghurt	2 tbsp shredded fresh mint,
150ml/5fl oz tomato juice	plus extra to garnish
4 spring onions, finely chopped	Few drops of Tabasco

Place the cucumber in a colander and sprinkle over 1 teaspoon salt. Set aside and leave to drain for 30 minutes, then rinse under cold running water and squeeze out any excess moisture with a clean tea towel.

Place the yoghurt, tomato juice, spring onions, garlic, stock and mint in a food processor and blend to a smooth purée – you may have to do this in batches. Stir in the cucumber and Tabasco, then season to taste and chill until very cold. To serve, ladle into bowls and garnish with the remaining mint.

GARLIC PURÉE SOUP

This soup is a great winter warmer that packs a subtle smoky garlic punch. You don't have to add the fromage frais if you're watching the calories, but you might then need a little extra stock to thin the soup down a little.

1 garlic bulb, separated into cloves	900ml/1½ pints chicken stock
1 tbsp olive oil	300ml/10fl oz low-fat fromage frais
2 onions, finely chopped	Salt and freshly ground black pepper
1 heaped tsp chopped fresh rosemary	2 tsp snipped fresh chives
350g/12oz potatoes, diced	
350g/12oz ripe tomatoes, peeled, seeded and chopped	

Preheat the oven to 200°C/400°F/Gas 6. Place the unpeeled garlic cloves in a very small roasting tin and roast for 25–30 minutes until lightly charred and completely tender. Leave to cool completely.

Heat the oil in a large pan. Add the onions, rosemary and potatoes and cook for about 5 minutes until softened. Add the tomatoes, pour in the stock, cover and simmer for 20 minutes, or until the potatoes are completely tender.

Peel the garlic cloves and stir into the soup. Leave to cool a little, then purée in batches in a food processor or with a hand-held liquidizer. Return to the pan and stir in the fromage frais, reserving some to garnish.

Season the soup to taste and reheat gently, without boiling. Ladle into bowls and add spoonfuls of the reserved fromage frais. Add a good grinding of black pepper and sprinkle the chives on top to serve.

SPANISH-STYLE MUSSEL SOUP

This soup has a wonderful rich flavour and you would never notice that it only uses one tablespoon of oil. Traditionally a good pinch of cinnamon is also added to the toast paste but I've decided to leave it out on this occasion.

2kg/4½ lb fresh mussels, cleaned	350g/12 oz ripe tomatoes, peeled,
300ml/10 fl oz dry white wine	seeded and chopped
3 large garlic cloves, peeled and halved	600ml/1 pint fish stock
Salt and freshly ground black pepper	2 slices unbleached white bread,
Good pinch saffron strands soaked	toasted and cubed
in 1 tbsp hot water	½ tsp cayenne pepper
1 tbsp olive oil	2 tbsp flat-leaf parsley leaves
1 large onion, chopped	3 tbsp brandy

Discard any cracked or opened mussels that do not close when tapped. Place the wine and 2 of the garlic cloves in a large pan, season with pepper and bring to the boil. Add the saffron and mussels, cover and cook over a high heat for 2–3 minutes, shaking the pan occasionally, until they have just opened – discard any that don't. Drain, reserving the cooking liquid, and discard the garlic. When the mussels are cool enough to handle, remove the meats from the shells, reserving some of the nicest looking whole ones for a garnish.

Heat the oil in the pan. Add the onion and cook for about 15 minutes until softened and golden, stirring occasionally. Add the tomatoes and cook for another few minutes until softened but still holding their colour. Pour in the stock and strain in the reserved mussel cooking liquid through a double layer of muslin to remove any sand and grit, then bring to a simmer.

Place the remaining garlic in a mini-blender with the toast, cayenne pepper, parsley and brandy and blend to a smooth paste, adding a little of the stock if necessary to help the mixture move around. Stir into the soup and cook for about 1 minute until thickened. Add the mussels, season to taste and just heat through. Ladle into bowls and garnish with the reserved whole mussels to serve.

Right: Green Summer Soup

ROAST YELLOW PEPPER SOUP

Grilled peppers have the most wonderful, smoky sweetness, which I just adore. Collect as much of the juices as possible as you peel them, as they really have a fantastic flavour.

4 yellow peppers	1 potato, diced
1 tbsp olive oil	1 tsp chopped fresh oregano
1 onion, finely chopped	900ml/1½ pints vegetable
2 garlic cloves, finely chopped	or chicken stock
1 red chilli, seeded and finely chopped	Salt and freshly ground black pepper

Preheat the grill. Place the peppers on the grill rack and grill for 20–30 minutes until the skins are blackened and blistered, turning frequently. Transfer to a polythene bag, secure with a knot and allow the peppers to steam in their own heat for 10 minutes. Remove from the bag, peel away the skin and remove the seeds, then roughly chop the flesh, reserving any juices.

Heat the oil in a large pan. Add the onion, garlic and chilli and cook for about 10 minutes until completely softened but not browned. Add the peppers with their juices, along with the potato, oregano and stock and bring to the boil. Reduce the heat and simmer for about 30 minutes until the potato is tender and the soup has thickened slightly.

Leave the soup to cool a little, then purée in batches in a food processor or with a hand-held liquidizer. To serve, reheat gently and season to taste. Ladle into bowls and add a grinding of black pepper to serve.

CHICKEN CONSOMMÉ

If chilled, this consommé will turn to jelly. If you want to serve it like this, just break it up with a fork and spoon into small, pretty cups. Garnish with plenty of chopped fresh herbs and you've got a soup fit for a king!

1.7 litres/3 pints chicken stock	2 egg whites, lightly whisked
450g/1lb ripe tomatoes, chopped	2 egg shells, crushed
1 large onion, chopped	Pinch of sugar
2 celery sticks, chopped	Dash of Madeira (optional)
2 carrots, chopped	Salt and freshly ground black pepper
1 bouquet garni	Vegetable hair (page 15), to garnish,
300g/10oz lean minced chicken	(optional)

Place the stock in a large pan with the tomatoes, onion, celery, carrots and bouquet garni and bring to the boil. Reduce the heat and simmer for 25–30 minutes until the vegetables are completely softened.

Stir the chicken mince into the stock, mixing until well combined, then add the egg whites and shells. Return to the boil, whisking continuously, then reduce the heat and simmer for another 30 minutes.

Strain the soup through a muslin-lined fine sieve and return to a clean pan. Season to taste and add the sugar and Madeira, if using. Ladle into bowls and garnish with small mounds of vegetable hair, if your diet allows.

PROVENÇAL SWEET PEPPER SOUP

This is a variation on the fiery, hot Provençal rouille sauce, traditionally served with fish soups. If you don't want to use double cream in the yellow pepper cream, replace it with Greek strained yoghurt – the contrast of colours is very dramatic.

4 large red peppers	½ tsp caraway seeds
2 slices day-old unbleached white bread	¼ tsp each cumin and coriander seeds
2 large garlic cloves, crushed	1 tbsp olive oil
2 red birds' eye chillies, seeded	900ml/1½ pints vegetable stock
and chopped	Yellow pepper cream (page 16),
Good handful fresh basil leaves	to garnish (optional)
Salt and freshly ground black pepper	

Preheat the grill. Place the peppers on the grill rack and grill for 20–30 minutes until blackened and blistered, turning regularly. Place in a polythene bag, secure with a knot and leave for 10 minutes. Remove from the bag, peel, seed and chop the flesh, reserving any juices.

Meanwhile, soak the bread in a little water for about 5 minutes, then squeeze out the excess moisture. Place in a food processor with the pepper flesh and any juices, garlic, chillies and basil. Season generously and blend to a purée.

Place the caraway, cumin and coriander seeds in a mortar and crush to a fine powder with a pestle. Heat the oil in a large pan. Stir in the ground spices and cook for 30 seconds, stirring. Pour in the stock and whisk in the pepper mixture until well combined. Season to taste and bring to a simmer to just warm through. Ladle into bowls, add a good grinding of black pepper and serve at once.

BLOODY MARY SOUP

This is actually more of a virgin Mary soup, but there is nothing to stop you adding a shot or two of vodka if it takes your fancy . . . I love this scattered with guacamole.

1 tbsp olive oil	3 tbsp Worcestershire sauce
450g/1lb ripe tomatoes, roughly	3 tbsp balsamic vinegar
chopped, or 450ml/15fl oz passata	Juice of 2 limes
(sieved tomatoes)	12 drops Tabasco sauce
4 spring onions, finely chopped	Celery salt and freshly ground black pepper
900ml/1½ pints tomato juice,	12–18 small ice cubes
preferably fresh	Guacamole (page 15), to garnish (optional)

Place the oil in a food processor and add the tomatoes, spring onions, tomato juice, Worcestershire sauce, balsamic vinegar, lime juice, Tabasco and plenty of celery salt and freshly ground black pepper. Blend until smooth – you may have to do this in batches – and pass through a fine sieve into a large bowl.

Cover the bowl with clingfilm and chill for at least 2 hours, but overnight is best. Ladle the soup into bowls and add a couple of ice cubes to each one. Scatter over the guacamole, if using, and serve ice cold.

Right: Roast Yellow Pepper Soup

FAST & EASY

These days, who has time to be stuck in the kitchen for hours preparing food? The recipes in this chapter have been devised with the busy cook in mind – all can be made in less than half an hour, some take far less. The ingredients have been kept to a minimum and many are already in a well-stocked kitchen, with the recipe requiring mostly cans and frozen foods. All recipes serve 4–6.

LETTUCE SOUP

This is a fantastic summer soup, but remember your finished soup will only taste as good as the lettuce you use. Buy it as fresh as possible for the best sweet, delicate flavour.

40g/1½ oz unsalted butter
2 shallots, finely chopped
1 large cos or butterhead lettuce, core removed and leaves finely shredded
4 tsp finely chopped fresh tarragon

Salt and freshly ground black pepper
900ml/1½ pints vegetable stock
150ml/5fl oz double cream
2 egg yolks

Melt the butter in a large pan. Add the shallots and cook gently for about 5 minutes until softened but not coloured. Stir in the lettuce and half of the tarragon and season generously, then cover and cook gently for 3–4 minutes, shaking the pan occasionally, until the lettuce has wilted.

Pour the stock into the pan and quickly bring to the boil. Reduce the heat and simmer gently for another 5 minutes.

Mix together the cream and egg yolks in a bowl. Add a ladleful of the hot soup and mix well to combine, then whisk back into the soup. Return to a gentle heat and cook for another minute or so until just heated through. Stir in the remaining tarragon and ladle into bowls to serve.

MIXED SEAFOOD SOUP

This is actually a bit of a cheat that I've learnt from the restaurant trade – apparently nobody ever notices . . .You can use any type of fish soup as the base, but obviously the better brands give the better result.

2 x 400g/14oz cans fish soup
900ml/1½ pints fish stock from a carton or made with a stock cube
Pinch saffron strands soaked in
1 tbsp hot water

450g/1lb mixed prepared seafood, such as shelled mussels, cooked peeled prawns and squid rings, thawed if frozen
4 tbsp brandy
Salt and freshly ground black pepper
Garlic croûtons (page 14 or shop bought), to serve

Place the fish soup in a pan with the stock, saffron and mixed seafood. Stir in the brandy and season to taste – you'll probably find you need to go easy on the salt.

Bring to the boil. Reduce the heat and simmer for about 5 minutes until heated through. Ladle into bowls and garnish with some garlic croûtons to serve – it's as simple as that!

SPRING COURGETTE SOUP

If you use the grating blade on a food processor to grate the courgettes, the preparation time for this soup will cut down to less than a minute. I like to make it in the spring when there is an abundance of herbs growing on my window sill, but it's great at any time of year.

2 tbsp olive oil
1 onion, finely chopped
675g/1½ lb courgettes, grated
Salt and freshly ground black pepper

900ml/1½ pints vegetable stock
4 heaped tbsp chopped fresh mixed chives, flat-leaf parsley, tarragon and chervil
Parmesan croûtes (page 14), to garnish

Heat the oil in a large pan. Add the onion and cook for a few minutes until softened but not coloured. Stir in the courgettes, season generously, cover and cook gently for 5 minutes until just tender.

Remove the lid from the pan, pour in the stock and bring to the boil. Reduce the heat, cover once more and simmer for another 10 minutes, or until just tender.

Stir in the herbs and purée in a food processor or with a hand-held liquidizer. Return to the pan, season to taste and reheat gently. Ladle into bowls and garnish with Parmesan croûtes to serve.

CHILLI BEAN SOUP

For an authentic Mexican flavour either garnish the soup bowls with spoonfuls of soured cream and a sprinkling of grated Cheddar, or pile tiny mounds of guacamole (page 15) on to tortilla chips and serve them alongside or float them on top.

2 tbsp sunflower oil
1 red onion, finely chopped
½ tsp each ground paprika, cumin and coriander
2 courgettes, cut into small pieces
100g/4oz baby sweetcorn, cut into small pieces

400g/14oz can mixed beans, drained and rinsed
400g/14oz can chopped tomatoes
2 tbsp bottled chilli and garlic sauce
600ml/1 pint vegetable stock
Salt and freshly ground black pepper

Heat the oil in a large pan. Add the onion and fry for a few minutes until softened. Add the paprika, cumin and coriander and cook for another minute, stirring. Add the courgettes and sweetcorn and stir-fry for 1–2 minutes until well combined.

Add the beans, tomatoes, chilli and garlic sauce and stock and bring to the boil. Reduce the heat and simmer for 6–8 minutes until slightly thickened. Season to taste and ladle into small bowls. Serve hot.

PEPERONATA SOUP

This is a version of the traditional Italian stew of peppers and tomatoes. To make this recipe even quicker, blend a couple of jars of mixed pepper antipasto with an equal quantity of stock.

4 tbsp extra virgin olive oil	600ml/1 pint vegetable or chicken stock
1 large onion, finely chopped	Salt and freshly ground black pepper
2 red and 2 yellow peppers,	Good pinch of sugar
seeded and chopped	1 tsp white wine vinegar
2 garlic cloves, crushed	Deep-fried basil leaves (page 15),
400g/14oz can chopped tomatoes	to garnish (optional)
in rich tomato juice	

Heat the oil in a large pan. Add the onion and peppers and cook over a fairly high heat for about 10 minutes until just tender and beginning to colour around the edges, stirring occasionally. Stir in the garlic and cook for another 1–2 minutes, stirring occasionally, then tip in the tomatoes and stock. Season to taste and bring to the boil. Reduce the heat and simmer for 10–15 minutes until the peppers are completely tender.

Purée in batches in a food processor or with a hand-held liquidizer. Return to a clean pan, stir in the sugar and vinegar and season to taste. Reheat gently, then ladle into bowls and garnish with the basil leaves, if using.

BAKED BEAN SOUP

Even the title of this soup sounds a bit strange, but I can assure you kids love it. I made it up one day when I was unexpectedly left with a bunch of children (the person responsible shall remain nameless) and it went down a treat.

450g/1lb pork sausages	400g/14oz can baked beans
2 tbsp sunflower oil	2 tsp Worcestershire sauce
1 large onion	Salt and freshly ground black pepper
900ml/1½ pints vegetable stock	Toasted cheese croûtes (page 14), to garnish
(from a cube is fine)	

Arrange the sausages on the grill rack and grill for a few minutes on each side until cooked through and lightly browned. Leave until cool enough to handle, then cut into small pieces.

Heat the oil in a large pan. Add the onion and cook for about 5 minutes until softened and lightly browned around the edges, then stir in the sausages.

Pour the stock into the pan. Add the beans and Worcestershire sauce, season to taste and bring to the boil. Reduce the heat and simmer gently for about 5 minutes until heated through. Ladle the soup into bowls and top each one with 3 toasted cheese croûtes to serve.

PRAWN AND CUCUMBER SOUP

You don't even need a cooker to make this soup, but if you've got the time it's worth sprinkling the cucumber with salt. Just set it aside for about 15 minutes, then rinse under cold running water and squeeze dry in a clean tea towel. This technique removes excess water and firms up the flesh.

225g/8oz cooked peeled prawns, minced,	2 tbsp chopped fresh dill,
plus 4–6 whole ones to garnish	plus 4–6 tiny sprigs to garnish
1 cucumber, halved, seeded and grated,	300ml/10fl oz still mineral water
plus 8–12 wafer-thin slices to garnish	600ml/1 pint natural yoghurt
	Salt and freshly ground black pepper

Place the prawns and cucumber in a large bowl and season generously. Stir in the dill and then pour in the water and yoghurt, mixing until well combined. Cover with clingfilm and chill for at least 2 hours, but overnight is best (or start with all the ingredients well chilled and serve it straight away).

When you are ready to serve, remove the clingfilm and give the soup a good stir. Season to taste and ladle into bowls. Garnish each bowl with 2 cucumber slices, slightly overlapping and topped with a prawn and a tiny dill sprig. Serve ice cold.

FIELD MUSHROOM SOUP

This soup doesn't take much longer than 20 minutes to make from start to finish. I find the lemon juice helps bring out the mushrooms' natural, savoury flavour. If you are trying to eat healthily, omit the cream and dilute the soup with a little extra stock if necessary – you'll find it's still pretty good.

675g/1½ lb field or open cup	2 tbsp plain flour
mushrooms, chopped	900ml/1½ pints vegetable stock
Juice of ½ lemon	Pinch of freshly grated nutmeg
50g/2oz unsalted butter	Salt and freshly ground black pepper
1 onion, chopped	150ml/5fl oz double cream
1 large garlic clove, crushed	

Sprinkle the mushrooms with the lemon juice. Melt the butter in a large pan. Add the onion and garlic and cook gently for a few minutes until softened but not coloured. Increase the heat, add the mushrooms and cook for 1–2 minutes, stirring. Stir in the flour and cook for another minute, stirring.

Gradually pour the stock into the pan. Add the nutmeg, season to taste and bring to the boil. Reduce the heat, cover and simmer gently for 10 minutes, or until the mushrooms are completely tender. Purée in a food processor or with a hand-held liquidizer. Return to a clean pan, season to taste and stir in the most of the cream, reserving a little to garnish. Reheat gently, ladle into bowls and add swirls of the reserved cream. Serve at once.

Right: Peperonata Soup

CHICKPEA AND GARLIC SOUP

This is a rich, intense spicy soup which reminds me of Moroccan holidays, and it can be made almost entirely from the storecupboard.

4 tbsp extra virgin olive oil, plus
extra to garnish
1 large onion, finely chopped
2 large garlic cloves, finely chopped
1 heaped tsp ground cumin
2 x 400g/14oz cans chickpeas,
drained and rinsed

900ml/1¹/₂ pints vegetable or
chicken stock
Salt and freshly ground black pepper
4 tbsp chopped fresh coriander, plus
extra leaves to garnish
Few drops of Tabasco
Juice of ¹/₂ lemon

Heat the oil in a large pan. Add the onion and garlic. Cook for about 5 minutes until well softened but not browned. Stir in the cumin and cook for a minute or so, stirring. Add the chickpeas and pour in the stock. Season generously and bring to the boil. Reduce the heat and simmer for 10 minutes, or until the flavours are well combined.

Place half of the soup in a food processor with the coriander and whizz to a purée. Return to the pan and stir until well combined. Heat through, add the Tabasco and lemon juice and season to taste. Ladle into bowls and garnish with swirls of olive oil and coriander leaves.

AVGOLEMONO SOUP

I first tasted this while on holidays in Greece and wasn't sure whether I liked it. However, over the years it has really grown on me and now it's one of the first things I want when I get off the plane.

2 tbsp olive oil
6 spring onions, finely chopped with white
and green parts separated
225g/8oz boneless, skinless chicken
breasts, cut into strips
100g/4oz long-grain rice

1.2 litres/2 pints chicken stock
Salt and freshly ground black pepper
2 eggs
Juice of 1 lemon
1 tbsp finely chopped fresh flat-leaf parsley

Heat the oil in a large pan. Add the white parts of the spring onions and stir-fry for 20 seconds, then tip in the chicken and cook for another 3–4 minutes, stirring frequently until the chicken is well sealed and lightly golden.

Stir in the rice and stock, season to taste and bring to the boil. Reduce the heat and simmer for 10–12 minutes until the rice is tender.

Meanwhile, beat the eggs in a bowl with the lemon juice. When the rice is tender, reduce the heat to as low as possible and whisk in the egg mixture. Simmer very gently for 1–2 minutes, whisking continuously until the egg is just cooked and not rubbery.

Remove the soup from the heat, season to taste and stir in the parsley. Ladle into bowls and scatter the green parts of the spring onions on top to serve.

BROCCOLI AND CHEDDAR SOUP

My mum used to make this all the time when we were young. We'd get a big bowl as soon as we got in from school on a cold winter's evening to keep us going until our dinner.

40g/1¹/₂ oz unsalted butter
1 large onion, finely chopped
225g/8oz potato, peeled and finely diced
Salt and freshly ground black pepper

900ml/1¹/₂ pints vegetable stock
675g/1¹/₂ lb broccoli head, well trimmed
and finely chopped
150g/5oz mature Cheddar, finely grated

Melt the butter in a large pan. Add the onion and cook for a few minutes until softened. Stir in the potato and season generously, then cover and cook gently for 10 minutes, shaking the pan occasionally until the potatoes are just tender.

Pour the stock into the pan and bring to the boil. Reduce the heat, add the broccoli and simmer for another 5 minutes, or until the broccoli is just tender.

Purée in batches in a food processor or with a hand-held liquidizer. Return to a clean pan, stir in the Cheddar and reheat gently for 1–2 minutes until just warmed through. Season to taste and ladle into bowls. Serve at once.

Above: Chickpea and Garlic Soup

WINTER VEGETABLE SOUP

This has to be one of easiest and most versatile soups I know – you don't even need to use any stock as the flavours are already powerful enough. You can vary the combination of vegetables you use, just keep the final weight to 675g/1½ lb.

50g/2oz unsalted butter
1 onion, finely chopped
2 small leeks, finely chopped
1 heaped tbsp freshly grated root ginger
Salt and freshly ground black pepper

450g/1lb carrots, grated
1 small parsnip, grated
1 small potato, peeled and grated
1 tbsp clear honey
Squeeze of lemon juice

Melt the butter in a large pan. Add the onion, leeks and ginger, season generously, cover and cook gently for 2–3 minutes until softened. Stir in the carrots, parsnip, potato and honey, cover again and cook gently for 5 minutes until softened.

Pour 900ml/1½ pints boiling water into the pan and return to the boil. Reduce the heat and simmer for another 8–10 minutes until all the vegetables are completely tender.

Purée the soup in a food processor or with a hand-held liquidizer. Return to a clean pan, season to taste, add a squeeze of lemon juice and reheat gently. Ladle into bowls and serve at once.

POTATO AND LEEK SOUP

You can now buy small, pencil-sized leeks in most major supermarkets, often in the organic section. I think they have a much better flavour and always seem to be less dirty, so keep a look out for them.

50g/2 oz unsalted butter
450g/1 lb small leeks, finely chopped
225g/8oz potatoes, peeled diced
1 heaped tsp fresh thyme leaves,
plus extra to garnish

Salt and freshly ground pepper
900ml/1½ pints chicken stock
150ml/5fl oz double cream

Melt the butter in a large pan. As soon as it foams, stir in the leeks and potatoes until well coated. Add the thyme and season generously, then press a buttered circle of parchment paper on top of the vegetables, cover the pan with a tight-fitting lid and cook gently for about 10 minutes, shaking the pan occasionally until the vegetables are softened but not coloured.

Remove the lid and paper from the pan, pour in the stock and bring to the boil. Reduce the heat and simmer for about 5 minutes until the potatoes are completely tender. Purée the soup in batches in a food processor or with a hand-held liquidizer. Pour back into a clean pan, season to taste and add the cream. Reheat gently, then ladle into bowls and garnish with thyme leaves. Serve at once.

Above: Mexican Avocado Soup

MEXICAN AVOCADO SOUP

This is a superb cold soup, which is excellent eaten with some Salsa fresca (page 12) piled in tiny mounds on to hot and spicy tortilla chips.

4 large, ripe avocados
6 spring onions, chopped
2 garlic cloves, chopped
1 large green chilli, chopped
2 tbsp chopped fresh coriander,
plus extra leaves to garnish

Grated rind and juice of 1 lime
450ml/15 fl oz vegetable or chicken stock
Fine sea salt and freshly ground
black pepper
300g/10 oz natural yoghurt
150ml/5 fl oz soured cream

Halve the avocados, remove the stones and scoop out the flesh. Place in a food processor with the spring onions, garlic, chilli, coriander, lime rind and juice and stock. Season generously and whizz to a purée. Transfer to a large bowl and stir in the yoghurt and most of the soured cream.

Cover with clingfilm and chill until very cold.

To serve, give the soup a good stir, season to taste and ladle into bowls. Garnish with small spoonfuls of the remaining soured cream, some seasoning and the coriander leaves. Serve at once.

PEA AND MINT SOUP

This soup is about as instant as you are ever going to get. It is good served both hot and cold, and the addition of the chilli gives it a surprising and pleasant kick.

50g/2oz unsalted butter
1 onion, finely chopped
2 garlic cloves, crushed
1 green chilli, seeded and finely chopped
450g/1lb frozen peas
Pinch of sugar

900ml/1½ pints vegetable or
chicken stock
Salt and freshly ground black pepper
2 tbsp chopped fresh mint, plus
extra leaves to garnish
Softly whipped cream, to garnish

Melt the butter in a large pan. Add the onion, garlic and chilli and cook for 3–4 minutes until softened but not coloured. Add the peas, sugar and stock, season generously and bring to the boil. Reduce the heat and simmer for 8 minutes until the peas are completely tender.

Add the mint to the soup and purée in a food processor or with a hand-held liquidizer. To serve, reheat gently and season to taste. Ladle into bowls and add swirls of cream and mint leaves to garnish.

CREAM OF SPINACH SOUP

Impressive enough to grace any dinner-party table, this soup can be made in the time it takes your guests to have a drink. You could also make it with a bag of frozen spinach and just cook it for a bit longer at the beginning.

2 tbsp olive oil
1 garlic clove, crushed
450g/1lb tender young spinach
Salt and freshly ground black pepper
Pinch freshly grated nutmeg

900ml/1½ pints vegetable stock
150ml/5fl oz double cream
2 egg yolks
6 tbsp freshly grated Parmesan
Bacon croûtons (page 14), to serve (optional)

Heat the oil in a large pan. Add the garlic and stir-fry for 20 seconds. Tip in the spinach and press it down well. Season generously and add the nutmeg. Cover and cook for a few minutes, shaking the pan occasionally until the spinach has wilted.

Pour the stock into the pan and bring to the boil. Reduce the heat and simmer for 2–3 minutes until all the flavours are well combined. Leave to cool a little, then purée in batches in a food processor or with a hand-held liquidizer. Return to the pan off the heat and season to taste.

Mix together the cream and egg yolks in a bowl and then beat in the Parmesan. Add a ladleful of the hot soup and mix well to combine, then whisk back into the soup. Return to a gentle heat and cook for another minute or so until just heated through. Ladle into bowls and scatter over the bacon croûtons to serve, if liked.

CLAM CHOWDER

This might look a bit more complicated than the other recipes in this chapter, but it really takes no time at all. If you can't get hold of fresh clams, simply use a jar of clams and rinse them well under cold running water before adding to the soup.

36 fresh clams, scrubbed and well rinsed
2 tbsp sunflower oil
100g/4oz streaky bacon lardons
4 small leeks, thinly sliced
2 celery sticks, sliced

2 potatoes, diced
900ml/1½ pints fish stock
400g/14oz can chopped tomatoes
Salt and freshly ground black pepper
2 heaped tbsp chopped fresh flat-leaf parsley

Discard any cracked or opened clams that do not close when tapped. Set aside the remaining clams.

Heat the oil in a large pan and fry the bacon for about 5 minutes until crispy. Add the leeks, celery and potatoes and cook for another 5 minutes or so until softened.

Meanwhile, place 150ml/5fl oz of the stock in a separate pan. Add the clams, cover and cook over a high heat for 3–4 minutes, shaking the pan occasionally until all the clams have opened. Discard any that don't open.

Drain the clams, reserving the cooking liquid. Leave to cool a little, then remove the meats from most of the shells, reserving the nicest looking ones for a garnish, if liked.

Add the tomatoes to the vegetable mixture, pour in the remaining 450ml/15fl oz stock and strain in the reserved clam cooking liquid through a double layer of muslin to remove any sand or grit.

Season to taste and bring to the boil. Reduce the heat and simmer for a further 8–10 minutes until the potatoes are tender but still holding their shape. Stir in the clams and parsley and just heat through. Ladle into bowls and garnish with the whole reserved clams to serve, if liked.

Right: Pea and Mint Soup

SUBSTANTIAL & FILLING

This is the chapter with the soups that are a meal in themselves. They may have long cooking times, yet many can simmer away on the back burner for hours, which simply helps to improve their flavour. They are also great for parties when you have to cater for large numbers – just scale up the recipe to the quantity you need to feed. All recipes serve 4–6.

CAWL

When I lived in England I always travelled back to Ireland on the ferry via Fishguard to Rosslare. There was a little café in Fishguard harbour that served the most delicious cawl, which we always demolished before the final leg of the journey home. I'm afraid it takes a bit of time to make, but it's worth it – I promise!

*1kg/2¼ lb gigot or rack lamb chops,
each 2.5cm/1in thick
2 onions, sliced
4 small leeks, sliced
6 carrots, sliced
1 small swede, chopped
Salt and freshly ground black pepper*

*675g/1½ lb potatoes, cut into large chunks
1.2 litres/2 pints chicken stock or water
1 tsp fresh thyme leaves
1 tbsp each softened butter and plain flour
1 tbsp each chopped fresh flat-leaf parsley
and chives*

Trim all the excess fat off the lamb and then render it down over a gentle heat in a large, deep pan with a tight-fitting lid. Discard the rendered-down pieces, leaving a layer of the melted fat behind. Toss the lamb chops into the pan and cook until lightly browned, turning occasionally, then transfer to a plate. Quickly toss the onions and leeks into the fat and then the carrots and swede.

Drain any excess fat out of the pan and layer the lamb, onions and leeks, carrots and swede, seasoning each layer. Lay the potatoes on top, so they can steam while the cawl cooks. Pour in the stock or water, season to taste, add the thyme and bring to the boil. Press a circle of buttered parchment paper down on top of the potatoes and cover with a lid. Leave to simmer for 1½–2 hours until the lamb is completely cooked.

When the cawl is cooked, carefully pour the cooking liquid into another pan. Skim off the grease and reheat the liquid. Melt the butter in a small pan. Stir in the flour and cook for 1–2 minutes on a low heat, stirring. Whisk into the liquid a little at a time until you have achieved the desired consistency. Season to taste and add the parsley and chives. Pour the liquid back into the pan with the lamb and potatoes and bring back to boiling point. Ladle into wide-rimmed bowls to serve.

SPICED BLACK BEAN SOUP

If you prefer a smooth soup, simply blend all the ingredients together just before serving, adding a little extra stock if necessary to get the desired consistency.

*2 large red peppers
2 tbsp olive oil
1 large onion, finely chopped
2 large garlic cloves, crushed
2 red Scotch bonnet chillies,
seeded and chopped
½ tsp each ground coriander and cumin
2 x 400g/14oz cans black beans,
drained and rinsed*

*900ml/1½ pints vegetable stock
Salt and freshly ground black pepper
Good handful fresh coriander leaves
Juice of 1 lime
Soured cream cooler (page 16),
to garnish (optional)*

Preheat the grill. Place the peppers on the grill rack and grill for 20–30 minutes until blackened and blistered, turning regularly. Place in a polythene bag, secure with a knot and allow to steam in their own heat for 10 minutes. Remove from the bag, peel, seed and dice the flesh, reserving any juices.

Meanwhile, heat the oil in a large pan. Add the onion, garlic and chillies and cook for about 5 minutes until softened. Stir in the ground coriander and cumin and cook for another minute or so, stirring.

Add the beans and stock to the pan, season generously and bring to the boil. Reduce the heat and simmer for 10 minutes, or until the beans are completely tender and heated through.

Place half of the soup in a food processor with the fresh coriander and whizz to a smooth purée. Return to the pan with the diced red peppers and any of their juices. Heat through and stir in the lime juice. Season to taste and ladle into bowls. Add a spoonful of the soured cream cooler and a good grinding of black pepper to serve.

SEAFOOD CHOWDER

You can also add a diced small parsnip and carrot to this soup to ring the changes. Don't be alarmed by the addition of the Chinese five-spice powder, the flavour really does work!

75g/3oz unsalted butter	1 onion, finely chopped
2 carrots, diced	350g/12oz firm white fish fillets,
1 potato, peeled and diced	skinned and any bones removed
2 celery sticks, diced, plus some	150ml/5fl oz fish stock
chopped leaves to garnish	100g/4oz cooked peeled large prawns
50g/2oz plain flour	150ml/5fl oz double cream
900ml/1½ pints milk	Pinch of Chinese five-spice powder
Salt and freshly ground black pepper	

Melt 25g/1oz of the butter in a large pan. Add the carrots, potato and celery, stirring to coat in the butter, then cover and cook gently for 15 minutes until tender, stirring once or twice.

Meanwhile, melt the remaining butter in a pan and remove from the heat. Stir in the flour, return to the heat and cook for 1–2 minutes, stirring. Gradually pour in the milk, whisking until smooth, and bring to the boil. Reduce the heat and simmer for 2–3 minutes, stirring occasionally. Season to taste and set aside.

Preheat the oven to 180°C/350°F/Gas 4. Spread the onion in a small roasting tin and arrange the fish on top. Season well and pour over about 4 tablespoons of the fish stock. Cover loosely with foil and bake for 10 minutes until just opaque. Leave to cool a little, then lift the fish off the onion mixture, break into bite-sized pieces and set aside. Reserve the onion mixture.

Add the white sauce, onion mixture and the remaining fish stock to the vegetables and gently bring to the boil, stirring well to combine. Reduce the heat, carefully fold in the fish and prawns and simmer for 1–2 minutes. Stir in the cream and Chinese five-spice powder and just heat through. Season, then ladle into bowls and garnish with celery leaves to serve.

CARIBBEAN SPLIT PEA SOUP

I have used canned yellow split peas in this recipe to speed up the cooking time. However, if you want you could replace them with dried peas – just soak 175g/6oz in plenty of water overnight and cook according to packet instructions, which usually takes 1½–2 hours.

2 tbsp sunflower oil	900ml/1½ pints vegetable stock
1 onion, finely chopped	400ml/14fl oz coconut milk
2 large garlic cloves, finely chopped	2 x 400g/14oz cans yellow split peas,
2 red Scotch bonnet chillies, seeded	drained
and finely chopped	Pinch light muscovado sugar
1 tsp fresh thyme leaves	Salt and freshly ground black pepper
2 tsp medium curry powder	Tropical salsa, to garnish (page 12)
1 tbsp ground paprika	

Heat the oil in a large pan. Add the onion, garlic, chillies and thyme and cook gently for 10 minutes until completely softened but not coloured. Stir in the curry powder and paprika and cook for another minute or so, stirring.

Pour in the stock, coconut milk, split peas and sugar. Season generously, then bring to the boil. Reduce the heat, cover and simmer for 15–20 minutes until the split peas are completely softened. Season to taste and ladle into bowls. Scatter some of the tropical salsa on top to serve.

CHICKEN GUMBO

Scotch bonnets are the hottest chillies in the world, so take care when preparing them. I often rub my hands in a little oil first which helps prevent the heat penetrating into the skin.

3 tbsp olive oil	2 green Scotch bonnet chillies,
1 large onion, finely chopped	seeded and finely chopped
4 celery sticks, finely chopped	1.2 litres/2 pints chicken stock
1 green pepper, seeded and finely chopped	400g/14oz can chopped tomatoes
225g/8oz fresh okra, cut into	in rich tomato juice
5mm/¼ in slices	1 bouquet garni
450g/1lb boneless and skinless	100g/4oz chorizo or keilbasa sausages,
chicken thighs, quartered	casings removed and sliced
2 tbsp seasoned plain flour	Salt and freshly ground black pepper
2 garlic cloves, finely chopped	

Heat the oil in a large pan. Add the onion, celery, green pepper and okra and cook gently for 10–15 minutes until the vegetables are completely tender but not coloured. Toss the chicken in the flour until well coated, then push the vegetables to one side of the pan and add the chicken. Stir-fry for a few minutes until the chicken is sealed and just golden.

Add the garlic and chillies to the pan and cook for another 1–2 minutes, stirring until everything is well combined. Pour in the stock and add the tomatoes, bouquet garni and sausages. Season to taste and bring to the boil. Reduce the heat and simmer for 25–30 minutes until the soup has reduced and thickened slightly. Ladle into bowls to serve.

Above: *Pumpkin and Melted Onion Soup*

PUMPKIN AND MELTED ONION SOUP

For an even richer version, stir in 100g/4oz of diced cheese, such as Gruyère or fontina, just before serving. It's a match made in heaven!

1kg/2¼ lb pumpkin or butternut squash	*2 tsp chopped fresh sage*
3 tbsp olive oil	*2 garlic cloves, finely chopped*
Salt and freshly ground black pepper	*900ml/1½ pints vegetable or chicken stock*
25g/1oz unsalted butter	*200ml/7fl oz crème fraîche*
2 large onions, finely chopped	*Parmesan croûtons (page 14), to garnish*

Preheat the oven to 230°C/475°F/Gas 9. Cut the pumpkin or squash into wedges, no more than 7.5cm/3in thick, and scoop out the seeds. Brush all over with 1 tablespoon of the oil and place on a roasting tray. Season generously and roast near the top of the oven for 45 minutes, or until caramelized. Leave until cool enough to handle, then scrape the flesh away from the skin – you should have about 450g/1lb.

Heat the remaining oil in a large pan with the butter. Add the onions and cook for 25 minutes until browned, stirring frequently. Add the sage and garlic and cook for another 5 minutes. Add the pumpkin and stock and simmer for 15–20 minutes until the pumpkin is tender.

Purée the soup in batches in a food processor or with a hand-held liquidizer. Return to the pan. Add most of the crème fraîche, season to taste and reheat gently. Ladle into bowls and top with spoonfuls of crème fraîche and the Parmesan croûtons to serve.

MOROCCAN HARIRA SOUP

Muslims traditionally sit down to enjoy a soup like this at the end of the day during the holy month of Ramadan, when not a bite of food can be consumed between sunrise and sunset. No wonder they need something so nourishing!

1 small cinnamon stick	*900ml/1½ pints chicken stock*
4 whole cloves	*400g/14oz can chopped tomatoes*
1 tsp each mustard, cumin and	*400g/14oz can chickpeas,*
coriander seeds	*drained and rinsed*
2 tbsp olive oil	*About 3 tbsp harissa (hot chilli paste)*
1 onion, chopped	*Salt and freshly ground black pepper*
350g/12oz lamb fillet, cut into	*1 tbsp each chopped fresh coriander*
bite-sized pieces	*and flat-leaf parsley*
1 tbsp plain flour	*Juice of ½ lemon*

Heat a small frying pan. Add the cinnamon stick, cloves and mustard, cumin and coriander seeds. Toast for 1–2 minutes until aromatic and slightly darkened in colour, tossing occasionally. Place the spices in a mini-blender or use a pestle and mortar and crush to a powder.

Heat the oil in a sauté pan. Add the onion and cook for 2–3 minutes until softened. Add the lamb and cook for a few minutes until sealed. Tip in the spices and flour, stirring to combine. Cook for a minute or so, then pour in the stock, add the tomatoes and simmer for 15–20 minutes until the lamb is completely tender.

Add the chickpeas and enough harissa to suit your taste and stir well. Season to taste and cook for few minutes until heated through. Stir in the herbs and lemon juice and ladle into bowls to serve.

CALDO VERDE

Normally made with a member of the cabbage family called *couve gallego*, this is Portugal's national dish. Curly kale is the nearest green to it that is readily available, but really any type of cabbage would do.

4 tbsp olive oil, plus extra to garnish	*200g/7oz chorizo sausages, casings*
1 large Spanish onion, halved	*removed and sliced*
and thinly sliced	*1.2 litres/2 pints chicken stock*
1 large red pepper, seeded and thinly sliced	*350g/12oz baby new potatoes, halved*
1 large yellow pepper, seeded	*Salt and freshly ground black pepper*
and thinly sliced	*450g/1lb curly kale, cored*
2 garlic cloves, crushed	*and finely shredded*

Heat the oil in a large pan. Add the onion, peppers and garlic and cook for about 10 minutes until the peppers are softened and beginning to caramelize. Stir in the chorizo and cook for another few minutes until sizzling, stirring occasionally. Pour in the stock and add the potatoes. Season generously and bring to the boil. Reduce the heat, cover and simmer for 15–20 minutes until the potatoes are completely tender.

Stir the curly kale into the pan, cover and cook for 3–4 minutes until wilted and completely tender. Season to taste and ladle into bowls. Add swirls of olive oil and serve hot.

CREAMY SALMON TARRAGON SOUP

This is so rich and tasty that it really is a meal in itself. I love to eat this with star-shaped pastry puffs floating on the top. Obviously you could use any cut of salmon but the escalopes save a lot of time because they cook so quickly.

1 tbsp sunflower oil	225ml/8fl oz dry white wine
25g/1oz unsalted butter	900ml/1½ pints fish stock
4 x 100g/4oz salmon escalopes	2 courgettes, halved and sliced
Salt and freshly ground black pepper	on the diagonal
2 large shallots, finely chopped	150ml/5fl oz double cream
1 small garlic clove, crushed	2 heaped tbsp finely chopped fresh tarragon
175g/6oz small button mushrooms, sliced	Pastry puffs (page 14), to garnish,
2 tbsp plain flour	(optional)

Heat the oil with the butter in a large pan. Season the salmon all over and add to the pan. Sear for 1–2 minutes on each side until lightly golden and just tender. Transfer to a plate and leave to cool a little, then roughly flake into smaller pieces.

Stir the shallots into the pan and cook for about 5 minutes until softened. Add the garlic and mushrooms, stirring until well coated. Season and stir-fry for a few minutes until the mushrooms are tender. Stir in the flour and cook for another minute or so, stirring constantly.

Pour the wine into the pan and boil rapidly for a few minutes, scraping the base with a wooden spoon. Pour in the stock and simmer for 25–30 minutes until slightly thickened and reduced.

Stir in the courgettes and cream and simmer for 2–3 minutes until the courgettes are just tender and the cream has slightly reduced. Return the salmon to the pan with the tarragon and just warm through. Season to taste and ladle into bowls. Garnish with the pastry shapes, if liked, to serve.

CARIBBEAN CRAB CALLALOO

Callaloo is a generic name given to the green leafy tops of the taro and malanga plants. If you can't get hold of it fresh, you can buy it in cans from West Indian grocers. Spinach or curly kale are good substitutes.

25g/1oz unsalted butter	1 tsp fresh thyme leaves
1 tbsp sunflower oil	900ml/1½ pints chicken or
100g/4oz streaky bacon lardons	vegetable stock
1 large onion, finely chopped	400ml/14fl oz coconut milk
1 red Scotch bonnet chilli, seeded	225g/8oz callaloo, finely shredded
and finely chopped	225g/8oz fresh or canned white crab meat
2 garlic cloves, crushed	Few drops Tabasco
350g/12oz potatoes, diced	Salt and freshly ground black pepper

Melt the butter in a large pan with the oil. Add the bacon and cook for about 5 minutes until crisp. Add the onion, chilli and garlic and cook gently for another 5 minutes until softened but not coloured.

Add the potatoes to the pan with the thyme, stock and coconut milk and bring to the boil. Reduce the heat and simmer for 10–15 minutes until the potatoes are completely tender.

Stir in the callaloo and cook for a few minutes, stirring occasionally until just beginning to wilt. Stir in the crab meat and Tabasco and season to taste. Simmer for a few minutes until the crab is heated through but the callaloo is still green. Ladle into bowls to serve.

MINESTRONE SOUP

You can use any type of small pasta shapes for this recipe, or just snap macaroni, spaghetti or tagliatelle into small pieces.

2 tbsp olive oil	1 heaped tbsp sun-dried tomato purée
100g/4oz bacon lardons	50g/2oz small dried pasta shapes,
2 small leeks, finely chopped	such as broken macaroni
2 carrots, finely chopped	Salt and freshly ground black pepper
2 celery sticks, finely sliced	4 Savoy cabbage leaves, thick stalks
2 garlic cloves, finely chopped	removed and leaves shredded
1 tsp fresh thyme leaves	1 small courgette, thinly sliced
900ml/1½ pints vegetable stock	6 tbsp Pesto (page 12)
400g/14oz can chopped tomatoes	14–16 ciabatta croûtes (page 14)

Heat the oil in a large pan. Add the bacon and cook for 5 minutes until golden. Add the leeks, carrots and celery and cook gently for about 5 minutes until softened but not browned. Add the garlic and thyme and cook for another 2–3 minutes without colouring. Stir in the stock, the tomatoes and tomato purée and bring to the boil. Add the pasta, season to taste, cover and simmer for 10 minutes, or until al dente.

Preheat the grill. Stir the cabbage into the soup and cook for a minute or so until just wilted, then add the courgette and cook for another minute until just tender. Stir in a heaped tablespoon of the pesto and season to taste. Ladle the soup into flameproof serving bowls. Spread the croûtes with the remaining pesto and arrange on top of the soup. Place under the grill until the pesto is bubbling. Serve at once.

FRENCH ONION SOUP

Cider instead of beer gives this classic French bistro soup a more subtle, mellow flavour. Use any type of Swiss cheese that is available or try an equal mixture of Gruyère and Parmesan, which also works well.

1 tbsp olive oil	*2 tbsp plain flour*
25g/1oz unsalted butter	*150ml/5fl oz vintage or other*
350g/12oz onions, thinly sliced	*good quality dry cider*
Salt and freshly ground black pepper	*2 tbsp Cognac or other brandy*
Good pinch of sugar	*12–18 croûtes (page 14)*
900ml/1½ pints chicken stock	*50g/2oz Gruyère cheese, finely grated*

Heat the oil with the butter in a large heavy-based pan. Add the onions, cover and cook gently for 15 minutes, stirring occasionally. Uncover, increase the heat and stir in ½ teaspoon salt and the sugar. Continue to cook for another 45 minutes, stirring frequently so the onions do not stick as they caramelize.

When the onions are a deep golden colour, pour the stock into a pan and bring to a simmer. Stir the flour into the onions and cook for 1–2 minutes, stirring. Gradually add the cider, stirring continuously, and then pour in the boiling stock, stirring to prevent any lumps from forming. Bring to the boil. Reduce the heat, cover and simmer for about 30 minutes until the onions are meltingly tender and the soup has thickened. Season to taste.

Just before serving, preheat the grill. Stir the Cognac or brandy into the soup and ladle into flameproof serving bowls. Float the croûtes on top and sprinkle over the Gruyère. Place under the grill until the cheese is melted and bubbling. Serve at once.

CULLEN SKINK

Make this very traditional Scottish soup and you'll see why its popularity has stood the test of time. I strongly recommend you use undyed smoked haddock for the best flavour and colour, rather than the bright yellow stuff.

350g/12oz floury potatoes,	*300ml/10fl oz fish or chicken stock*
cut into chunks	*300ml/10fl oz milk*
50g/2oz unsalted butter	*1 heaped tbsp snipped fresh chives*
Salt and freshly ground black pepper	*150ml/5fl oz double cream*
1 large onion, chopped	
450g/1lb natural smoked haddock,	
cut into large pieces	

Place the potatoes in a pan of boiling salted water, cover and simmer for 15–20 minutes until completely tender. Drain and mash well, then beat in half of the butter and season to taste.

Heat the remaining butter in a large pan. Add the onion and cook gently for about 5 minutes until softened but not coloured. Add the haddock and pour 450ml/15fl oz water on top, then simmer for 10 minutes until the fish is just cooked through and flakes easily.

Lift out the pieces of fish with a slotted spoon, transfer to a plate and leave until cool enough to handle, then roughly flake, discarding any skin and bones.

Stir the mashed potato into the cooking liquid, mixing until well combined. Pour in the stock and milk and bring to the boil. Quickly reduce the heat and simmer for 3–4 minutes until heated through and well combined, stirring occasionally.

Stir the flaked fish, chives and cream into the pan and cook gently for a few minutes until heated through. Season to taste, then ladle into bowls and serve at once.

Right: French Onion Soup

HUNGARIAN GOULASH SOUP

If you don't want to use pork fillet, beef or chicken work just as well, or for a vegetarian version, simply replace the meat with a 400g/14oz can of mixed beans that have been rinsed and drained.

2 tbsp sunflower oil
1 red onion, chopped
2 red peppers, seeded and finely chopped
1 large garlic clove, crushed
100g/4oz button mushrooms, sliced
350g/12oz pork fillet, cut into small strips
1 heaped tbsp hot paprika, plus extra for dusting

1 tbsp seasoned plain flour
900ml/1½ pints chicken or vegetable stock
400g/14oz can chopped tomatoes
1 heaped tbsp tomato purée
Salt and freshly ground black pepper
100g/4oz dried pasta bows (farfalle)
Soured cream and chopped fresh flat-leaf parsley, to garnish

Heat the oil in a large pan. Stir in the onion and peppers and cook for 2–3 minutes until softened. Stir in the garlic and mushrooms and cook over a high heat for a few minutes until the mushrooms are tender.

Meanwhile, toss the pork strips in the paprika and seasoned flour until coated. Push the mushroom mixture to the side of the pan and add the pork. Stir-fry for a few minutes until just tender and lightly browned.

Pour the stock into the pan and add the tomatoes and tomato purée. Season to taste and bring to the boil. Reduce the heat, stir in the pasta bows and simmer for another 10–15 minutes until the pasta is *al dente*. Ladle into bowls and garnish with a swirl of soured cream, a dusting of paprika and a sprinkling of parsley to serve.

WINTER LENTIL AND VEGETABLE SOUP

This soup certainly won't break the bank. Don't be afraid to leave out a vegetable if you don't have it to hand, or to substitute one for another.

2 tbsp olive oil
100g/4oz smoked streaky bacon lardons
1 large onion, finely chopped
2 small leeks, thinly sliced
2 carrots, chopped
2 celery sticks, chopped
2 garlic cloves, finely chopped
1.2 litres/2 pints vegetable stock

4 large, ripe tomatoes, peeled and roughly chopped
100g/4oz red lentils
1 bouquet garni
Salt and freshly ground black pepper
Juice of ½ lemon
2 heaped tbsp roughly chopped fresh flat-leaf parsley

Heat the oil in a large pan. Add the bacon and cook for about 5 minutes until crisp, then push to one side of the pan and add the onion and leeks. Cook gently for a few minutes until softened. Stir in the carrots, celery and garlic and cook for another 4–5 minutes, stirring occasionally, without allowing the vegetables to colour.

Pour the stock into the pan and add the tomatoes, lentils and bouquet garni. Bring to the boil, then reduce the heat, cover and simmer gently for 30 minutes, or until the lentils are completely tender. Season to taste and stir in the lemon juice and parsley, then ladle into bowls and serve at once.

PEA AND HAM SOUP

For a real treat, use the freshest of peas and new potatoes and all you'll need is a hunk of moist, crusty bread for a complete meal.

50g/2oz unsalted butter
1 onion, finely chopped
225g/8oz new potatoes, scrubbed and diced
350g/12oz fresh or frozen peas
900ml/1½ pints chicken stock
Salt and freshly ground black pepper

225g/8oz cooked smoked ham, cut into small dice
150ml/5fl oz double cream
1 egg yolk
1 tbsp each chopped fresh flat-leaf parsley and mint

Melt the butter in a large pan. Add the onion and potatoes and cook gently for about 10 minutes until the potatoes are almost tender but not coloured.

Stir the peas and stock into the pan, season to taste and bring to the boil. Reduce the heat and simmer for 4–5 minutes until the peas are completely tender.

Roughly purée in a food processor or with a hand-held liquidizer and pour back into the pan. Stir in the ham and reheat gently.

Mix together the cream, egg yolk and herbs in a bowl and whisk in a ladleful of the hot soup. Whisk into the soup and simmer for another 3–4 minutes, without boiling, until warmed through, stirring occasionally. Season to taste and ladle into bowls. Serve at once.

TUSCAN BEAN SOUP

This soup is especially delicious when made with really sweet, ripe, juicy tomatoes. If it is not the right time of the year for them, replace with two 400g/14oz cans of chopped tomatoes.

100g/4oz dried cannellini beans, soaked overnight
4 tbsp extra virgin olive oil
2 large garlic cloves, finely chopped
1kg/2½ lb plum tomatoes, peeled, seeded and diced

1 heaped tsp chopped fresh oregano
Good pinch of sugar
Salt and freshly ground black pepper
600ml/1 pint vegetable or chicken stock
2 tbsp shredded fresh basil
4–6 tbsp Pesto (page 12)

Place the beans in a large pan and cover with water. Slowly bring to the boil and boil vigorously for 10 minutes. Reduce the heat and simmer for about an hour until the beans are soft but not collapsed. Drain and rinse under cold running water.

Heat the olive oil in a large heavy-based pan. Add the garlic and cook over a gentle heat for 2–3 minutes, being careful not to let it brown. Add the tomatoes, oregano, sugar and seasoning and bring to the boil. Reduce the heat and simmer for about 15 minutes until thickened.

Pour in the stock, season to taste and return to the boil. Reduce the heat and simmer gently for another 15–20 minutes until the tomatoes are thoroughly combined and the soup has thickened slightly. Stir in the cooked beans and basil and just heat through. Ladle into bowls, add a swirl of pesto to each one and serve at once.

Right: Tuscan Bean Soup

RECIPE INDEX

ACKNOWLEDGEMENTS

This book is dedicated to Derek, for all his help, patience and support. With special thanks to my mum for all the time spent cleaning up after my recipe testing sessions. Particular thanks to Debbie Major, who gave the manuscript a final read and offered invaluable comments. Thanks also to Laura Washburn and Maggie Ramsay at Weidenfeld & Nicolson and to Emma Patmore for her great food styling. Also, to all the food writers and chefs who have inspired me over the years. Lastly, a big thank you to Mitzie Wilson, my first boss at BBC *Good Food* magazine, for believing in me and sending me on my way.

First published in the United Kingdom in 1999 by Weidenfeld & Nicolson

Text copyright © Weidenfeld & Nicolson 1999
Photographs © Robin Matthews
Design and layout copyright © Weidenfeld & Nicolson 1999

A CIP catalogue record for this book is available from the British Library

ISBN 0297 82513 5

Stylist: Roisin Nield
Home economist: Emma Patmore

Printed and bound in Italy

Illustrated Division
The Orion Publishing Group
Wellington House
125 Strand
London WC2R 0BB